KITCHENS

CREATIVE
IDEAS
FOR
YOUR
HOME

KITCHENS

The Knapp Press · PUBLISHERS · LOS ANGELES

The publisher would like to thank the designers, homeowners, and manufacturers whose willing cooperation made this project possible. Thanks are also due Williams-Sonoma, Inc., for providing accessories for many of the kitchens photographed for this book.

Published by The Knapp Press
5900 Wilshire Boulevard, Los Angeles, California 90036

Project editor: Sarah Lifton
Book and jacket design: Paula Schlosser
Page layout: Linda Robertson
Writers: Kirsten Grimstad, Diana Rico

Cover photographs:

Front cover photo by Jessie Walker, kitchen design by Mary Jane Pappas and Carol Belz

Back cover upper left: photo by Diane Padys; upper right: photo by William P. Steele, kitchen design by Charles Morris Mount; middle left: photo by Diane Padys, kitchen design by Mary Fisher Knott; middle right: photo by Jessie Walker, kitchen design by Mary Jane and Bruce Colglazier Pappas; lower right: photo by Diane Padys, kitchen design by Donald E. Silvers

Library of Congress Cataloging in Publication Data

Main entry under title:

Kitchens.

    (Creative ideas for your home)
    Includes index.
    1. Kitchens—Remodeling. I. Knapp
    Press. II. Series.
TH4816.K59 1984   643′.3   84-7883
ISBN 0-89535-137-4

Printed and bound in the United States of America

10 9 8 7 6 5 4 3 2 1

For Bud

Mary Fisher Knott, who served as consultant on this book, has been a professional kitchen planner since 1963. During her lengthy career, she has designed more than 3,500 kitchens and received 8 professional awards. Employed by public utilities companies for 12 years, she pioneered home modernization and energy conservation programs for residential customers, and since 1974 has designed kitchens and interiors independently for numerous private, commercial, and professional clients across the country. She regularly conducts kitchen-planning seminars throughout the western United States and lectures on topics related to home improvement. The author of magazine articles and various publications about home planning, she appears frequently on radio and television.

CONTENTS

FOREWORD

Every year the editors of HOME magazine review thousands of photographs and visit hundreds of kitchens. We see traditional kitchens, country kitchens, contemporary kitchens, high-tech kitchens, and many that fall into that catch-all category called eclectic. We see cabinets made of wood, metal, plastic laminate (often accented with wood detailing and in luscious colors and interesting textures) and, increasingly, we're seeing cabinets finished in high-gloss lacquer. We see counters surfaced in ceramic tile, in granite, marble, butcher block, stainless steel and, of course, more laminate. Floors boast earthy quarry tile or eye-catching ceramic tile, lustrous wood or durable slate, soft carpeting or comfortable, versatile vinyl. Yet out of all these kitchens, no more than 40 are selected for publication each year—which raises a question we're often asked: What makes a kitchen *special,* not just worthy of being photographed and published by HOME but the successful realization of a dream?

In a nutshell, we look for an artful combination of form and function. Good looks alone won't do it, nor will superb efficiency. Beyond that, there are many factors, each of them important in its own way. We look for the unique—special storage features, unusual materials, the personal touches of a homeowner who not only appreciates good design but who obviously enjoys cooking and wants his or her kitchen to celebrate that pleasure. We strive for a broad geographical sweep: The cabinets in that Santa Fe house may be just what a Connecticut homeowner chooses to duplicate for his rustic home. And—an essential consideration—we always look at whether the expense involved represents good value.

Our readers' reactions support HOME's approach to kitchen coverage. In search of ideas for their own homes, they eagerly devour features and photos presenting well-designed, one-of-a-kind kitchens. At the same time, however, a kitchen remodeling is clearly a chance for each of them to express his or her individual tastes and personality. No one really wants to duplicate exactly a kitchen from the pages of a magazine—or a book, for that matter—regardless of how innovative it

may be. So what we try to do is present ideas that the homeowner can adapt for his own home. If you have a marvelous collection of antique splatterware or copper pots, for example, you may want to add display cases or incorporate open storage into the traditional-style kitchen that just caught your eye. Or, if your hate clutter and live in a house with a fantastic view that demands to be the focal point of the room, you may consider the choices and opt for a version of the all-white laminate kitchen featured in the last issue of your favorite magazine. But if, like most of us, you're attracted to all sorts of looks, colors, and materials, you're probably going to want to explore all the alternatives before going ahead with your remodeling project.

More often than not, however, a kitchen remodeling is a complicated proposition and usually too big a job for the average do-it-yourselfer to tackle alone, even aided by a battery of books and magazines. That's where professional help comes in. In planning the project, an array of professionals is at your disposal, most of whom can make one or more aspects of the process go more smoothly and ensure the results you want. One professional is not like another, however, as many people have discovered to their dismay; members of different professions have different orientations. And, frankly, individual abilities in any field are as disparate as the people involved. While at best many professionals know their fields well, there is no substitute for an ongoing dialogue between the kitchen designer and an informed, participating homeowner-client. And at worst, there are many professionals who plan or install kitchens, yet really don't know much about how a good kitchen should work and look.

Anyone designing a kitchen should know how to cook and should always consider that the primary function of the room is to produce meals in the most efficient manner possible. Veteran New York kitchen designer Charles Morris Mount always makes a point of cooking with his clients as part of his regular consultation process. Former chef and Los Angeles kitchen designer Donald E. Silvers always prepares a dinner party with his client in the new kitchen, showing him or her how to take best advantage of the kitchen's new configuration.

An architect, on the other hand, may be concerned primarily with a clean, unbroken line, possibly at the expense of efficiency and storage needs. An interior designer may get caught up in the aesthetic considerations and lose sight of the functional. A cabinet dealer may be trying to sell you more "boxes" than you actually need. A contractor may be in the habit of doing a certain type of kitchen, rather than fitting it to your needs. Although many of these people are well equipped to produce exactly the kitchen you've dreamed of, no professional, not even the new breed of kitchen planner/ spatial consultant, can be expected to redo your kitchen successfully without input from you, the chief cook and bottle washer.

Knowing what is available is a major part of your kitchen-planning education, and it pays you to keep up with the latest developments, since technology in the field is galloping along at a breakneck pace. Are you aware, for example, that there is now a refrigerator/ freezer with a built-in ice cream maker? That you can purchase refrigerators and freezers that are standard cabinet depth (no ugly protrusions to mar a clean look) and can be fitted with virtually any front panel to fit any decor? That the new induction cooktops offer the utmost in safety and ease of maintenance? That you can basically design a custom cooktop to suit your particular cooking needs?

Technological advances haven't been confined to appliances, either. New space-age materials are also now on the market. A new process has produced a plastic laminate with the surface color throughout, eliminating the often unattractive black line at the joints. Another laminate in tambour form can be curved around cabinetry. A synthetic material called Corian duplicates the look of marble and can be cut and molded into an infinite number of shapes, making a seamless juncture of backsplash and counter, for example. Warm-toned fluorescent lamps can now light your kitchen for less than the cost of incandescent bulbs, but without the cold, eyestrain-producing effect of the old-style flu-

orescents. Carefully designed European-style cabinet interiors can be retrofitted into inefficient but perfectly serviceable older cabinetry.

More than once, however, I've done careful research in a product category only to have a contractor or dealer tell me that there is no such product as the one I know exists. If this happens to you, it usually means one of two things—that you are better informed than the professional who sells or deals with such items or, more simply, that he can't get what you're asking for and will try to sell you something else. In the end, it's up to you to explore all your options and stand firm about what you want.

Clearly, planning a new kitchen can be a daunting prospect. But to ease the process along, we've developed *Kitchens,* which is an invaluable tool to help you tackle the project with confidence. In the pages that follow, you'll find everything from exciting idea-generating photos and text to the hard information necessary to make the right decisions. And it's this very blend of creative ideas and good, solid, up-to-the-minute information that distinguishes *Kitchens* from other books on the subject. Cutting through the often difficult technical jargon prevalent in other publications, *Kitchens* presents the facts you need to begin a remodeling project, explained in a way that you, the concerned homeowner, can comprehend and organized to help you readily apply the information to your own situation. And, to bring these basic theories into the world of reality, more than 400 photographs present inspired—and inspiring—examples of kitchen design.

Just as its title promises, chapter 1, Kitchen Basics, provides invaluable background information about all of the elements that must be considered in putting together a smooth-functioning, attractive kitchen. Here you will learn about the general considerations of kitchen design, from layout to style, from walls, ceilings, and floors to lighting, cabinetry and, of course, appliances.

Chapter 2 takes you through the preplanning stages, helping you to apply the elements of good kitchen design to your own kitchen, enabling you to evaluate your own needs. Is poor layout one of the reasons the kitchen is so hard to keep neat? Do cleanup chores get in the way of cooking? Does your desire to display attractive serving pieces incline you to generous open storage, or are you a neatnik who wants everything hidden away behind doors? Is the kitchen really set up for the kind of cooking you do? What sorts of professionals can best help you plan and execute the kitchen you really want? What major considerations can keep costs down?

Once you've gotten used to thinking about all the areas in which your kitchen needs improvement, it's time to get specific—to develop solutions to the problems you face in your own kitchen every day. And to make that step easier, the next three chapters are devoted to small, medium-sized, and large kitchens, respectively. Each of these chapters approaches the design of a specific-sized kitchen in a consolidated fashion, addressing the challenges inherent in remodeling each size kitchen. In a small kitchen, for instance, increasing storage and work space is apt to be of prime consideration. In a medium-sized kitchen, only one or two areas of the room's function may need to be reworked. In a large kitchen, it may be hard to create a feeling of coziness and, from a practical point of view, it may be difficult to use the space effectively and locate all major appliances within the optimum configuration.

As a general frame of reference, we've decided to consider a small kitchen to be one that contains less than 120 square feet; a medium-sized kitchen to be between 120 and 170 square feet; and a large one to be over 170 square feet. These are rough figures; odd shapes and certain architectural features—lots of doorways, for example—could make a kitchen with fairly generous dimensions take on the attributes of a medium-sized kitchen. And, too, it's important to bear in mind the fact that many of the suggestions for solving the problems of a particular-sized-kitchen—a bay extension to a small kitchen, for example—may mean that the new kitchen actually becomes a larger one. You may also find ideas in another chapter that you'd like

to adapt for your own kitchen. So no matter what size kitchen you're currently saddled with, it's worthwhile to review all the sections, since there is an inevitable overflow of ideas from one chapter to another.

Having studied your kitchen and considered the alternatives, the time inevitably comes when theory must be transformed into action, when visions of a dream kitchen must be translated into everyday reality. At this stage you should be able to approach your professional team as an equal partner, not just as the person who signs the checks. And, importantly, you should also be able to eliminate any nasty surprises from the whole process. Chapter 6, Plan into Action, sets out the steps you'll need to take in order to implement your plan. You'll learn how to draw a floor plan, create a color board specifying colors and materials, hire a professional, get building permits, schedule inspections, and set up a temporary kitchen.

The final section of the book—Close-ups and Options—provides close-up photographs of materials, products, and features, from hardware to sun rooms, with capsule discussions of the alternatives to help you put the custom touches on the new kitchen you're planning. And to assist you in finding the products, we've also provided a list of major manufacturers, who will be able to direct you to dealers in your area.

As I've said, I've looked at many kitchens. But the kitchen I'm scrutinizing most closely at the moment is my own. It's a classic 1939 job with hideous green cabinetry, outdated avocado-green appliances, a tacky linoleum floor, mismatched windows, and four doorways creating a horrendous traffic pattern. I can honestly say that reading the manuscript for this book has helped me tremendously as I face the prospect of remodeling my own kitchen. What better endorsement can I give?

Olivia Buehl
Editor, HOME magazine

KITCHENS

CHAPTER 1

Kitchen Basics

A step-saving L-shaped layout promotes efficient traffic patterns in this country-style kitchen, which features hand-painted tiles and bleached oak cabinetry.

Today's kitchen has evolved by quantum leaps from its recent predecessors. Professionals have devoted their energies to designing kitchens that are efficient and comfortable, while manufacturers offer many practical and aesthetic options in their products. The result? Lovely, functional rooms that reduce fatigue while maximizing the rewarding, creative aspects of kitchen activity. The basic elements of beautiful, well-designed kitchens are described and shown here to help you plan a kitchen best suited to your needs.

Essentials of Layout

- *What constitutes an efficient layout?*

A well-conceived kitchen layout allows an easy flow of work from the storage area (centered around the refrigerator) to the preparation area (centered around the sink) to the cooking and serving area (centered around the range). These three areas are the corners of the basic work triangle, ideally located beyond the flow of through-traffic. Connecting the three work centers by uninterrupted countertop gives you maximum space to prepare a meal. Two important considerations for counter space allotment are (1) how can uninterrupted space be achieved? and (2) what is the optimum space for work efficiency? Excessive distances between work centers may turn cooking into a marathon and send you shopping for track shoes. Optimal total distance connecting work centers varies from 15 to 22 feet: 5 to 7 feet from refrigerator to sink, 5 to 6 feet from sink to range, and 5 to 9 feet from range to refrigerator.

The triangle itself is placed within the larger configuration of the kitchen, which can take any one of the following shapes, with variations. A *U-shaped* kitchen has appliances and cabinets occupying three continuous walls and/or countertops. In an *L-shaped* kitchen, the same features take up two adjoining counters and/or walls, while in a *galley* or *corridor* kitchen, the elements are on opposite counters or walls. The *one-wall* kitchen works in extremely compact spaces and, with careful planning, can be attractive and convenient.

The U-shaped kitchen generally delivers maximum efficiency because of the generous amount of unbroken countertop and storage between work centers and be-

cause through-traffic bypasses the work triangle. The L-shaped kitchen gets the runner-up award for its continuous work surface on two walls. However, this layout is more vulnerable to interference from traffic and it may also be difficult to keep work centers from being too spread out. Third in order of desirability is the one-wall kitchen, which possesses the virtue of saving steps, but rarely provides adequate counter surface. The galley kitchen offers the most limited possibilities, not only because traffic passes directly through the work triangle, but also because its work centers are not connected by continuous countertop.

Fortunately, you are not confined to your kitchen's original layout, even if you do not plan to move or add walls. Islands and peninsulas have become popular and versatile ways to change basic kitchen shape without altering wall structure. An island is a freestanding unit usually placed to pull the work centers together while diverting traffic away from the work triangle. In addition to its countertop and storage merits, an island can house a cooktop, range, sink, dishwasher, snack bar, and other features. An island requires 42-inch clearance on all sides so that more than one person can move about freely even when someone is bending to reach some remotely placed item. A peninsula can serve the same functions as an island and takes less space because the peninsula extends from the wall or adjacent counter, eliminating the need for clearance on that side. A peninsula often serves to separate the kitchen work area from adjacent eating area or family room. By simply adding a peninsula, a humble one-wall kitchen can be turned into a proud, effective L-shaped kitchen. By installing an island, traffic can be routed away from the work triangle, endowing the kitchen with a more efficient layout. And if your remodeling agenda includes adding or removing walls to consolidate rooms, a whole new world of layout options becomes available.

Workhorse Work Centers

- *How can work centers be organized most efficiently?*

The food storage center, which includes refrigerator, freezer, and pantry or larder, is best located near the entry so that groceries can be whisked out of the

Even a seemingly inadequate space can accommodate an island with the help of some resourceful modifications. Here, angling the full-height cabinetry and island corners brings about the required clearance while enhancing the flow of traffic.

The uncommon shape of this peninsula—harboring both the cooktop and cleanup center—adds visual interest while gracefully distinguishing the cooking area from the dining area.

car and into their proper places. As a general rule of thumb, counter space should extend at least 18 inches between the refrigerator and sink, with the refrigerator door opening toward the sink and counter. If a large pantry is wanted, and if space and budget allow, the pantry can be the walk-in kind. With more limited needs and means, the pantry can be a cabinet with narrow shelves for molasses, soup cans, pet food, spices, and assorted canned and packaged staples. Base cabinets can be outfitted with vented bins for handy storage of fresh fruits and vegetables. A tin-lined drawer is an excellent storage place for bread.

Between refrigerator and sink is the ideal location for mixing activities and supplies. Here you have easy access to milk and eggs from the refrigerator, sugar and flour from the pantry, and water from the sink. This intermediate station can house mixer and blender, baking sheets, custard cups, cake pans, measuring utensils, plus various hand tools such as cookie cutters, egg beater, sugar scoop, spatulas, and rolling pin. Located between the refrigerator and sink, a mixing center needs to be at least 36 inches wide.

Next along the food preparation assembly line comes the sink, used in preparation (such as washing and peeling vegetables) and for cleanup. Because of this dual role, a good place for the sink is between the refrigerator and the range. It is nice to have a window above the sink; whether it overlooks your garden, neighborhood, or street, it makes for a pleasant change from sink scenery. For food preparation at the sink area, include cutting surfaces (either countertop or pull-out boards) and a garbage disposer. Remember to plan storage space for the colander, salad spinner, vegetable peeler, paring knives, orange squeezer, and other crucial hand tools. For the sink's cleanup function, allocate space for a dishwasher, trash compactor and/or trash receptacle, and cleaning supplies. Depending on the configuration of the kitchen, the sink requires at least 12 inches of counter space on each side.

The last link in this chain of work centers is the cooking and serving area, which, if possible, should be situated in proximity to the eating area. An island or peninsula can be designed for both cooking and dining, thus preventing wasted steps between cooktop and dinner table. With a cooktop on an island, you will need a minimum of 12 inches on each side and at the back to allow for jutting pot handles. At least 21 inches of work surface is needed adjoining a range. Depending on your individual needs, the cooking area can include a combination range or a cooktop and separate built-in ovens. Make sure the cooking center has storage space for the coffeemaker, roasting pan, ladle, knives,

pancake turner, waffle iron, salt and pepper shakers, and pots and pans. For serving convenience, you can store dinnerware and table linens in this area or, to facilitate cleanup, house dishes within handy reach of the dishwasher.

Bear in mind that space and counter allowances ultimately depend on the size and layout of your kitchen. One room's minimum is another room's maximum, and the suggested allowances given here are simply basic guidelines, which can be adapted as necessary.

The Bare Facts about Appliances

- *How do you choose appliances?*

A kitchen's overall efficiency also depends on the quality and appropriateness of the appliances within the work triangle. What appliances you need and what you have room for are the two primary considerations, and depending on these factors, you may choose separate built-in appliances or compact, consolidated units. Obviously, the more space you have—or will have after remodeling—the more appliance options you can consider. A fact-finding mission to an appliance dealer will give you an idea of what's available, but it's best to consult a kitchen planner for specifics and before making any purchases.

In addition to quality, suitability—and price—you should also consider how the manufacturer's service and warranty compare to others. What maintenance and repair services are available for the appliances you have selected? In this time of escalating fuel costs, it is also wise to consider energy ratings. A yellow energy guide label is affixed to most refrigerators, freezers, dishwashers, and ranges and gives an estimate of the yearly cost of operation compared to the equivalent models of other manufacturers.

Cold Storage Options

- *What features are available in refrigeration devices?*

A serviceable refrigerator and freezer are, of course, essential to a well-designed kitchen, and the size (in cubic feet) that your family requires may best be determined by assessing the shortcomings of your present model. A total of 12 cubic feet (refrigerator and freezer) is considered adequate for the average two-person family; add two cubic feet for each additional family member. In addition, you may want more or less than the average allotment, depending on your lifestyle. If you like to keep large quantities of perishable foods on hand, a large-capacity refrigerator is a good choice. Some individuals, however, find that a small, 12-cubic-foot model is quite adequate for keeping ice trays, beverages, and small amounts of food. The other extreme is the busy wage-earner who prepares a week's worth of meals during the weekend and freezes them in individual serving containers, ready to pop into the oven after a hard day at work. Such individuals and families require large freezers. Analyze your cold-food storage needs well in advance of purchasing an appliance. The kitchen space available will also influence what you choose. Before purchasing it, measure the exact height, width, and depth available for the appliance.

Size is not the only factor to consider, of course. Equally important is the arrangement of shelves and storage containers, which varies in different models. And you also have the choice of a freestanding refrigerator that comes encased in enamel, ready for service wherever you place it, or a built-in unit, which must be housed in a cabinet. The freestanding unit is generally 30 inches deep, while the built-in model is 24 inches deep. Both types are available in a side-by-side style (refrigerator and freezer door placed vertically) and a standard model (doors placed horizontally). Appliances are available with the freezer on the top or on the bottom. The standard style comes in 28- to 36-inch widths; the side-by-side unit comes in widths of 30 to 48 inches. Side-by-side models are quite popular, although the shelf width is fairly narrow, which makes it hard to retrieve items from distant corners. And side-by-side models do not easily hold large trays of hors d'oeuvres, desserts, or pastry dough.

The refrigerator's intended position in the kitchen will determine on which side the door is hinged. The door should open toward the counter so there is a handy place to put things taken out. If counter space is to the left of the refrigerator, purchase a right-hinged unit and vice versa. Some models feature a door that can be hinged on either side, so it can be converted from left to right or the reverse if the kitchen layout changes.

Side-by-side models always have the refrigerator door hinged on the right and the freezer door hinged on the left. If your countertop arrangement demands a left-hinged unit, you may want to buy a standard horizontal model. If your refrigerator will be located in a corner, remember that the refrigerator door will only have clearance to open about 90 degrees, which may affect access to meat and vegetable bins. The design of some models accounts for this need and in others it does not.

Special features available on today's refrigerators include self-defrosting capability, which adds convenience at the cost of additional energy consumption. Many models also offer cold water and ice cube dispensers on the outside of the freezer door. Because it isn't necessary to open the freezer door each time ice cubes must be replenished, this feature conserves energy and, if summertime brings troops of children wanting a drink of water, it's very handy, as well. Outside access to water and ice is also useful for those who entertain frequently. Automatic ice cube dispensers require hook-up to a water line, which may affect the refrigerator's location in the kitchen.

If space allows, consider adding a separate freezer to supply frozen vegetables and fruit all year round or to store the side of beef so appealing to your thrifty nature. Freezers come in a standard upright model or a chest type (rarely used in kitchens) that opens from the top. When buying an upright model, be sure that it is hinged on the correct side for your kitchen layout. It is wise to select a model with adjustable shelves large enough for a turkey, baking sheets with butter horns lined up, a soup kettle filled with chili for the Monday night football potluck, or any other special storage needs.

A small, undercounter model may fill the bill if only a small amount of additional freezer space is needed. For some families, the small separate freezer takes care of all frozen-food storage so that space required for a standard combination freezer-refrigerator can be used to house a large-capacity full refrigerator. If kitchen floor space is limited, perhaps you can locate the spare freezer in the garage or basement.

Sinks and Their Cleanup Companions

• *What options are available in today's sinks?*

First decide how many sink compartments you need. Sinks come in single-, double-, and triple-compartment models. A single-compartment sink requires the smallest counter area and is the least expensive type of sink. If it is used mainly to wash vegetables, with the dishwasher handling most cleanup duties, then a single-compartment sink can do the job. A single sink with

Tilt-out storage keeps cleaning supplies close at hand by this three-compartment sink designed for large cleanup chores.

disposer is not workable, however, because while dirty dishes are soaking, you cannot use the disposer. If you must have a single sink, get one with a small, separate compartment for garbage disposal.

Without a dishwasher, a double-compartment sink is a necessity, in order for food preparation and cleanup to take place simultaneously. Even with a dishwasher, most people prefer a two-compartment sink.

A three-compartment sink is handy for the aftermath of large gatherings or dinner parties, allowing three-way distribution of fragile china, crystal pieces, and pots and pans. Unfortunately, a three-compartment sink is more likely to fit into the generous dimensions of a large kitchen than into a small one, and insufficient counter space may prohibit this option.

Sinks are manufactured with many variations in size, shape, and proportions. To accommodate roasting pans and large stockpots, you will find an extra-deep compartment a welcome option. Another variation is a double-compartment sink with one large compartment for dishes, pots, and pans, and another small compartment, with disposer, for vegetable preparation. European manufacturers make circular sinks in one- and two-compartment models. Some sinks are equipped with hardwood inserts that fit over the sink compartment to extend countertop space. A hole in the wood slab allows you to whisk discards into the disposer below.

Sinks are finished in either stainless steel or porcelain enamel on cast iron or steel. Both porcelain and steel are durable and stain resistant. Porcelain enamel finishes come in a spectrum of colors to please practically any decorative palette, while stainless steel may complement other accents in your color scheme, which may dictate your choice. Be sure to get a heavy 18-gauge steel sink, if you do choose to go stainless. Some models come with stainless steel extenders for draining dishes. This feature is particularly desirable in a kitchen with butcher block countertops because butcher block tends to darken and deteriorate around the sink area from the effects of water.

One final consideration in purchasing a sink is how you want it mounted on the countertop. A self-rimming sink mounts on top of the counter and forms its own finished rim, overlapping the countertop. The other kind is set into the counter, its edges finished by the trim of the countertop material or by a steel rim, although a self-rimming sink can be set into the counter if tile or other material is used to create a finishing trim. Some countertop materials, such as laminated plastic, require a self-rimming sink because a suitable finishing trim is not available. If setting your sink into the counter is important to you, then select a countertop material such as tile, which provides a finished edge. In ordering a sink, be sure to specify the number of holes needed for faucets (single lever or separate hot and cold levers) and other accessories such as water filter, instant hot water, spray nozzle, and, if applicable, the air gap of the dishwasher.

A stainless steel sink equipped with extenders protects vulnerable butcher block from the harmful effects of moisture.

The sink's allies in the cleanup function include the garbage disposer, trash compactor, and dishwasher. Garbage disposers are available with either continuous-feed or batch-feed operation, and they vary in size and noise level. Some units have an insulation jacket to muffle the racket. Trash compactors are convenient and useful, especially for those who live in rural areas where there is no trash collection. A compactor can instantaneously transform overflowing bags of bottles, cans, and boxes into one neat little package for easy disposal. A compactor fits under the counter, preferably in the vicinity of the sink. Size is usually influenced by the available space; units come 12, 15, or 18 inches wide. Compacted trash has little air among the squashed items, however, and is therefore considerably heavier than a regular bag of garbage. Not surprisingly, the largest units produce the heaviest trash, which may influence your choice if you have to haul the full bags downstairs or any great distance.

The dishwasher, that modern-age miracle of drudgery relief, comes in two basic styles—the portable type that rolls out from its stow-away spot to hook up at the sink, and the common built-in type that requires its own plumbing hook-up. There is also a convertible unit, which rolls around portable-fashion until circumstances warrant a permanent installation. At that time,

you simply remove the top, slide it into its new, permanent position, and have the plumber and electrician hook it up.

Dishwashers come in a standard width—24 inches—although a recent exception, an 18-inch-wide compact unit, is now available for tight squeezes. The interior rack arrangements vary from one manufacturer to another, and should be scrutinized for their ability to accommodate your tall, oddly shaped, oversized pieces in addition to everyday dinnerware. Also, check the number of water sources your prospective purchase offers. Models have one, two, or three sources; three provide the best distribution of water throughout the dishwasher interior. Another salient feature to consider is the filter that removes food particles during the wash cycle and prevents them from clogging the drain. The filter should be positioned so that it can be removed easily for cleaning. Some models also offer a soft-foods disposer, which allows you to put dirty dishes directly into the dishwasher without prerinsing them. This feature saves energy that otherwise goes down the drain with your hot rinse water. Some models come equipped with a power-saver cycle that conserves energy by letting the dishes dry without using the heating element.

The latest brave new world dishwasher offers a built-in sensing device, which determines the cleansing

This self-rimming sink set into a butcher block counter exhibits masterful detailing. Note that its faucet and sundry accessories require the provision of four holes.

requirements of each particular load and adjusts the water supply and drying time accordingly. This futuristic development maximizes energy conservation in the washing and drying cycles.

Cooking Appliance Cornucopia

• *What are the considerations in selecting cooking equipment?*

In recent years, the old, single-unit freestanding range that delivered Mother's finest sourdough rye has given way to a variety of new age cooking appliances. You can still get the standard range with a cooktop and one or two ovens housed in a single casing with a variety of exterior finishes. Today, a single-oven range may be a drop-in model, which fits right into kitchen cabinetry and therefore does not require finished sides. Double-oven ranges are usually available in what is called *bi-level style*—that is, a single oven with cooktop and another oven above. This style is available in freestanding models only.

A combination range offers space-saving advantages. If this is not of concern in your kitchen, you have the option of a separate built-in cooktop and built-in ovens. The cooktop is installed right in the counter surface. The advantage of separate units is that you can position them for your greatest convenience—for example, cooktop on the island in easy serving range of the eating area, ovens over next to the baking center. Cooktops come equipped with two to six burners, plus cooking surfaces, griddles, and grills; ovens are available with self-cleaning catalytic (chemical) or pyrolytic (high-heat) features.

Choosing gas or electric cooking may depend on the cost of each type of energy in your area; this information is available from your local utility companies. If you select gas, be aware that most gas cooking equipment on the market is equipped with pilotless electronic ignition systems that will reduce operational costs. If electric cooking is your preference, an appealing cooktop alternative is magnetic induction. Induction cooktops, available in smooth-surface, single-unit models or as decorative tiles mounted in the countertop, cook food in iron or steel pots by creating an electromagnetic field between the cooktop and the pot. The units themselves do not get hot, and when they are not on cooking detail, they can fill in as extra counter surface. Because most people do not own exclusively iron or iron alloy cook-

This advanced-technology cooktop features the smooth decorative surface of Fasar tiles for magnetic induction cooking, rounded out by a pair of conventional gas burners.

ware, it is wise to supplement an induction cooking system with two standard gas or electric burners or surfaces for use with other cookware.

In addition to standard electric and induction cooking, there are two other kinds of electric cooking, microwave and convection. In microwave cooking, radio waves penetrate the food, causing the water molecules within to move, creating heat. Microwave ovens are available in two types, 110-volt and 240-volt models. The 110-volt models are generally plugged into a wall outlet, while the 240-volt units are built in, often in combination with a conventional or convection oven. When considering a microwave oven, it is important to keep in mind that metal cookware cannot be used for microwave cooking. If you have cookware that is suitable for microwave cooking or are willing to buy new cookware, the next consideration is what size microwave is best for the kind of cooking you do. Examine the features of the microwave to see if any or all would be useful in your kitchen. Microwave ovens should be placed adjacent to counter space, either above, below, or next to it, and at a height that will enable you to place dishes inside and remove them with ease.

Heat-retardant ceramic tile surrounds and insulates this heat-producing commercial cooktop. Overhead, a heavy-duty customized ventilation system discharges fumes.

Convection ovens, also available in 110-volt or 240-volt models, are found most often in combination with a conventional oven. In convection cooking, a fan circulates the heated air, which helps to speed up the baking process and evenly distribute the heat.

Now, a word about commercial equipment for home cooking. These units have become popular with home gourmet chefs because they offer up to twelve burners (an impractical choice, however, for home use) with plenty of space for oversized pots. Similarly, the oven dimensions can accommodate several roasts or a batch of pizzas all at once. For home use, however, commercial units require special adaptations in the kitchen. Because they generate so much heat, they must be installed in cavities lined with heat- and fire-retardant material such as brick or stone. Commercial units also require customized ventilation systems to handle the burden of cooking fumes they produce. And, because they are deeper than standard counter depth, commercial ranges will jut out from the counters unless the base cabinets and counters are tailored to fit. Unless they have pilotless ignition, their mere presence burdens the air conditioning system—an unfortunate side

effect of the continually burning gas pilot. And many units are simply too large to clear standard-size doors.

Homeowners often spend a great deal of time deciding which appliances to purchase but forget to consider a ventilating system. There are two basic types of systems. An updraft type sucks fumes up through an exhaust fan installed in a hood or overhead cabinet, venting them to the outside. A down-draft system draws the fumes down through the appliance cabinet and exhausts them through a vent to the outside. The significant difference between these two systems is that the down-draft type does not need a range hood or even a nearby wall for the exhaust fan. That makes a particularly appealing choice for a cooktop installed in an island or peninsula where you wish to keep the flow of space unobstructed. An updraft system, however, conveniently hides down-lighting for the cooktop.

All ventilation systems are rated according to the cubic feet of air per minute (CFM) they exhaust. The CFM rating required for your cooktop depends on several factors. A wall-mounted hood has the backsplash and wall to help direct the fumes up into its motor; it usually comes with a rating of 450 to 650 CFMs. For an island or peninsula installation, a stronger motor is needed to draw the air. For a peninsula, a 650 to 900 CFM vent is suitable; for an island, 900 to 1,000 CFMs. If you include a separate griddle or grill, separate venting is needed for it as well. If ductwork has to travel a particularly long distance or make one or more 90-degree turns to get to the outside, this must be taken into account—additional motor power will probably be necessary. In the event that fumes cannot be carried to the outside for some reason, the alternative is a self-venting hood, which sucks the air up through charcoal filters before exhausting it back into the kitchen.

The Finishing Touch

• *What decorative considerations apply to the purchase of new appliances?*

Your appliances not only do their various jobs—they also make visual statement, and their finish can be coordinated with the overall decorating plan. Appliances today come in a rainbow palette of enamel colors (two new colors are platinum and silver gray), in snappy black glass, in stainless steel, or in brushed chrome. If you are not replacing all your old appliances, you can have an appliance-refinishing firm repaint or

A ceiling-mounted hood such as this requires extra motor power in order to capture cooking odors.

This king-sized custom hood ventilates fumes and smoke from a grill and commercial cooktop.

A hoodless residential cooktop with down-draft ventilation provides an unbroken line overhead, which is especially desirable in an open-plan kitchen.

This wall-mounted hood services the needs of a residential cooktop while blending with the decorative theme.

A refrigerator in gleaming black—refinished to design specification—extends the color scheme.

Wood trim fronts on the dishwasher and trash compactor blend these common appliances gracefully into a unified bank of base cabinets.

reenamel your old equipment to coordinate with the look of the new kitchen.

With the help of trim kits—metal frames that attach fitted panels to the faces of the appliances—appliances can also blend in with the surrounding cabinetry. If you want this option, you must specify trim kits when you order your appliances. Your cabinetmaker or dealer will then provide the panels to match your cabinets.

Some Principles of Style

• *What gives a kitchen a distinctive look?*

A well-planned, integrated style is what makes the difference between an ordinary, efficient kitchen and the knockout designs featured in the pages of decorating magazines and in designers' showrooms. And aesthetic considerations are as crucial to a kitchen's harmony as are well-functioning appliances and an efficient layout. The goal is a unified blend of colors, patterns, materials, and furnishings that expresses a certain mood or style, be it austere and functional, dramatic, or cozy and welcoming. No matter how pleasing single elements may seem in their native context—say, the charming antique country stove you saw at the flea market or those smart lacquer-finish cabinets at the Italian design showroom—unless they are combined just so, the result can be as dissonant as flutes and foghorns. With these caveats out of the way, what are some guidelines for creating a successful decor?

The many kitchens represented on these pages bear testimony to the wide variety of choices that confront the hopeful remodeler. The tried-and-true darling of many designers today is basic white, executed in sleek lines and with natural wood accents. This sort of functional simplicity is only one interpretation of contemporary styling, however, which can incorporate a full gamut of colors, textures, and materials. Other general styles include *traditional*, a polished, more formal approach, with wood cabinetry and either understated or ornate detailing, and *country*, a warm, informal look that often includes weathered boards, bricks, and old-fashioned floral patterns in fabrics and wall coverings.

There are also a number of period styles that may be particularly suited to the architectural character of your home. An eighteenth-century Massachusetts farmhouse may welcome an early American kitchen with maple cabinets, wrought iron pulls, and a wood-burning stove. A converted loft in Soho with exposed structural elements is a good candidate for a neo-modern, high-tech approach. Turn-of-the-century style with leaded glass windows, highly polished brass fixtures, marble countertop, and a tin ceiling offers another distinctive period approach.

Finally, there is the catch-all category of eclectic styling, which fuses periods, themes, moods in an uninhibited harmony of old and new, simple and elegant, whimsical and practical. Eclectic styling relies on basic design principles to create a pleasing sense of order with diverse elements.

Classic Contemporary

• *What are the characteristic features of a contemporary kitchen?*

A contemporary kitchen is defined by a look of spare elegance enhancing functional efficiency. Smooth natural woods, laminated plastics, glass, chrome, stainless steel, and other contemporary materials create a refined and understated mood. Pattern emerges from the materials themselves—in the subtle outline of drawers and shelves, the geometry of tile grout—with the curved line of the dining table or countertop adding a

The understated simplicity of laminated plastic cabinetry, Corian counters, and geometric lines exemplifies the contemporary look in kitchen design.

This kitchen, with painted wood cabinets, expresses the traditional style of the house in its subtle palette and restrained decorative elements.

sculptural effect. All shapes follow a precise, linear, controlled geometric rhythm. Clearly, in a room with these restrained and disciplined qualities, clutter would not be welcome. The palette can range from quiet pastels to bright, clear, resonant tones, and this style can be used to good effect in kitchens of any size.

Traditional Balance

• *What essential qualities and detailing characterize traditional decor?*

At the opposite end of the stylistic spectrum is the traditional look, a formal design mode that whispers the virtues of order, moderation, and tranquillity. The style embraces a wide range of materials, colors, and finishes, from muted, pastel painted cabinetry to the deep, rich, and hand-rubbed look of mahogany. Symmetrical balance of elements and clearly defined architectural rhythms contribute to a mood of strength and grace; handsome wood cabinets have elegant moldings and brass pulls. The traditional style can carry rich embellishments such as classical columns, arches, etched glass, dark wood beams overhead, and ornate fixtures. This style works to best advantage in a room of moderate size.

The Country Casual Style

• *What qualities and features can be combined to create a country ambience?*

While the traditional kitchen borrows from the polished, formal, predictable drawing room, the country kitchen evokes the unpretentious charm of an earlier way of life. It is reminiscent of rural roots, of the beck-

Rich wood finishes, exposed beams, copper utensils on display, and an etched glass cabinet door prove that the country style can possess plenty of polish.

The contemporary lines of the sun room and the more traditional look of raised-panel wood cabinetry produce a surprisingly unified effect in this eclectically styled kitchen.

oning aroma of a simmering stockpot and crusty bread straight out of the oven. The beauty of a country kitchen lies in its rough-hewn rather than sophisticated character—the stone hearth, unfinished beams overhead, brick or tongue-and-groove on the walls, wide wood-plank flooring, and unadorned brass hardware. The materials themselves can be heavy, even massive, yet the overall feeling is bright and cheerful with the addition of colorful checked gingham on the table, a jaunty hooked rug, and flowering plants lining the windows. Furnishings and accessories come straight from Grandmother's attic or from a well-stocked country flea market—a sturdy oak breakfront to display pewter dinnerware, a handsome tin milk can or even a spinning wheel for a favorite corner, and on the mantel lots of old brass and copper cookware and utensils.

The Artful Mélange

• *What is eclectic style, and how is it different from a hodgepodge?*

An eclectic kitchen strives for harmony in diversity. It can be a melting pot of cultures, traditions, and moods, achieving its effect through a graceful interplay among the elements. Unlike a traditional, country, or period kitchen, an eclectic kitchen does not march to the sound of a single drummer, but is spontaneous and unpredictable. In an eclectic kitchen, you might find easygoing butcher block hand in hand with a stately column and ornate hardware. Or a contemporary glass and wood table atop a needlepoint rug. Glamorous cabinet designs from the showrooms of Milan may serve as a backdrop for family heirlooms. The eclectic grab bag gives generous rein to the many-sided personality—the functionally efficient, ultra-modern, as well as the nostalgic, the urbane, and the natural.

Does this mean that anything goes? No, indeed. In the absence of a cultural, traditional, or period theme, color plays the crucial role in uniting the elements. Mix and match to your heart's content, but keep your choices within a fairly controlled palette—one or two compatible colors with another contrasting color used sparingly for accents. The same rule applies to patterns: stick to designs that go well together, that repeat each other in size of pattern, in shape of pattern, or in the configuration itself. Strict discipline in the choice of pattern and palette supports the freedom of the eclectic mode. When it comes to textures, keep them scaled to the size of the room (a large room can take heavier textures) and consistent with the decor. Smooth textures suggest a formal mood; rough textures suggest relaxed informality.

Cabinets Exemplar

• *What factors should be considered in selecting new cabinets or restyling old ones?*

By virtue of the amount of space it occupies, cabinetry sets the dominant theme in any kitchen. Your choice of decorative style will determine the style of cabinetry and vice versa.

Cabinets are available in a multitude of styles, finishes, and materials: hardwood, soft wood, low-cost particle board with woodgrain veneer, laminated plastic, glossy lacquer finish, natural wood, and wood with dark finish. There are cabinets with wood frame doors and leaded glass panes, a variety of moldings and pulls, exposed hardware, and many other features.

Depending on your needs, you can purchase factory-built, modular units, which come prefinished in standard sizes, or custom cabinets, which can be made to any size and design specifications. Modular base cabinets measure 24 inches deep, 34½ inches high, and 9 to 48 inches wide, when ordered from a domestic manufacturer. Base cabinets, which support your counter surface and hold pots and pans, may have shelves or drawers or a combination of both, and may be ordered with special storage features, such as roll-out shelves, lazy Susans, etc. Modular overhead cabinets come 12 to 15 inches deep, 12 to 42 inches high, and 9 to 48 inches wide, and can be ordered with adjustable shelving, swing-out spice storage, storage racks on doors, and other special features.

Overhead cabinets allow for some subtle differences in the treatment of the angle where the wall joins the ceiling. Cabinets can extend up to the ceiling, providing maximum interior storage space. Or, a 12-inch space can be left open above the cabinets for an airy feeling and space to display rarely used decorative pieces or creeping plants. A third choice is a soffit, or dropped portion of the ceiling, between the cabinets and ceiling. A soffit is usually the same material as walls or ceiling and can remain hollow or conceal ductwork, electrical wiring, or other unsightly fixtures, or add to the room's lighting system.

Rounding out the array of cabinet options are full-

Roll-out shelves in base cabinets bring the contents of difficult-to-reach recesses gliding out for easy retrieval.

Swing-out spice storage increases cabinet capacity while maintaining order.

A margin of space left open above overhead cabinets contributes a feeling of spaciousness and provides an attractive location for display of decorative objects and plants.

height, floor-to-ceiling units (usually 24 inches deep) for housing tall appliances, food, the broom and other cleanup supplies, or dishes. The space above built-in tall appliances can be put to good service as a home for serving trays, platters, baking sheets, and baking racks.

Imported European modular units in standard metric sizes are also available in this country. Your cabinet dealer can assist in translating millimeters to feet and inches. Special adaptation may be required in combining European cabinetry with domestically manufactured appliances because the toe-kick allowance varies—approximately 6 inches for European cabinetry, 4 inches for domestic cabinets and appliances. Many cabinet manufacturers—both European and domestic—also offer modular units in custom sizes. This enables you to tailor your cabinet arrangement to the measurements of your kitchen and layout rather than the reverse.

For unusual needs and effects, custom-made cabinets from a cabinetmaker are often the best solution. You select the construction material, finish, hardware, and any accessories, such as heavy-duty extension glides for roll-out shelves in base cabinets. Free of the restrictions of standard sizes, custom cabinetry can give a unique look to your kitchen, as well as solve architectural or space problems.

A wealth of special features is available in both custom and modular cabinets to tailor kitchen storage to your needs. Useful options include partitioned storage for serving trays and cookie sheets, pull-out bins for trash storage and dog food, a pop-up caddy for your mixer, and door racks for cans and spices. Lazy Susan or half-round pull-out shelves provide handy access to remote corners. Be sure to allow an opening large enough to get items in and out without difficulty. If a corner proves too great a problem for convenient storage, give it up and see if this space would be useful as a closet or storage area opening into the room at its back. Such problem corners can sometimes be made into handy closets for adjacent rooms.

Recipes for Walls

• *What are the possibilities for wall covering?*

Like the cabinetry, wall treatment plays a vital role in determining the style and mood of a kitchen. In addition to paint and wallpaper, the most familiar wall treatments, a wide selection of materials, textures, and finishes ranging from wood paneling, brick, or stone to cork, ceramic tile, textured plaster, and mirrored or laminate surfaces can be used for various effects—to enlarge a room with airiness and light or pull together a cavernous room, infusing it with warmth and making it homey. Wall treatment can also significantly muffle the sounds of shrieking children or brass quintets emanating from the stereo center in the neighboring family room. And, of course, durability and ease of maintenance are among the most important considerations in selecting a wall treatment.

The soffit above the cabinetry conceals indirect perimeter lighting, which dramatizes appealing architectural features.

The narrow space above the ovens is a convenient location for partitioned storage of baking sheets and serving trays.

This versatile full-height cabinet houses not only the refrigerator-freezer but a broom closet and wine storage as well.

Lazy Susan shelves offer an effective answer to the ubiquitous dilemma of inaccessible corner cabinets.

*A contrasting color scheme opens the ceiling up visually,
offsetting the dark tones of the walnut cabinetry and
tile counters.*

Light tones of textured fabric wall covering create a warm yet airy feeling in this contemporary kitchen.

In selecting color for your walls, first think of the effect of color value in light absorption and reflection. White reflects up to 89 percent of the available light while black reflects as little as 2 percent. Light values on the walls are cheerful, and they increase the room's apparent size. Because of the amount of light reflected, light-colored walls require less artificial illumination. The smooth surfaces of paint, wallpaper, and tile increase light reflection. Light values also seem to recede visually; combined with inconspicuous textures, for instance, light walls create a feeling of spaciousness.

Dark color values on the walls decrease the room's apparent size, creating a mood ranging from restful to melancholy. Warm, dark colors combined with noticeable textures such as wood or brick give a feeling of

enclosure. Sharply contrasting colors draw attention to and emphasize the contours of architectural features, furniture, and other objects.

These principles also apply to the color value of wallpaper. In addition, vertical symmetrical patterns, subdued, cool colors, or rich, full-bodied colors combined with smooth surfaces contribute a feeling of formal balance. Asymmetrical patterns, horizontal lines, warm colors or clear, bright colors combined with a blend of textures create a mood of informality. Small patterns and muted colors tend to be quiet and restful while spirited patterns and bright, contrasting colors are vivacious. Bold patterns and colors attract the eye and dominate the space, overshadowing furniture and people; discreet patterns and colors have the reverse effect.

As for the practical consequences, high-gloss or semi-gloss enamel paint is more durable and easier to clean than a flat latex covering. However, for walls that are in less than pristine condition, more effective cover-

A feeling of friendly informality derives from a spirited wallpaper design—extended in tone and arrangement of tiles—set off against the line and color of the cabinetry.

up is provided by other types of wall covering. Textured wallpaper, wood or plastic laminate paneling, and ceramic tiles, for instance, are excellent concealers. Wallpapers are no longer limited to paper, but come in vinyl, vinyl paper, metallic paper, veneers of wood, cork, or grass, or fabric sealed with vinyl finish to repel moisture and grease. Soft materials such as fabric, cork, or soft woods absorb sound, but they are certainly not a good choice for the backsplash area or anywhere near the cooktop because these materials cannot be scrubbed the way ceramic tile or plastic laminate can be.

The Obliging Floor

• *Can a kitchen floor be beautiful, resilient, and require only minimal maintenance?*

Because the floor is a comparatively unbroken expanse, it makes a strong visual statement, shaping the character of a room. Yet kitchen floors receive so much wear and tear that they need to be sufficiently durable to hold up under rough treatment. Kitchen floors are also targets for all kinds of spills, and so must stand up to frequent cleaning. At the same time, they ideally should offer some measure of comfort underfoot. The secret to comfort is resiliency, but the other qualities most often are associated with hard surfaces. So selecting a suitable kitchen floor covering can be a series of trade-offs.

A resilient surface cushions impact and reduces fatigue while also keeping down the noise level. Rubber tiles, vinyl tiles, vinyl asbestos tiles, vinyl sheet goods, and carpeting all fall into the category of good, resilient surfaces, with carpeting the most resilient and the best choice for noise reduction.

If your home is an upstairs apartment or condominium, a carpeted kitchen floor can minimize disturbance to those below. For homes in cold climates, a carpeted kitchen adds an important layer of insulation, helping keep the room warm. Properly treated to repel moisture, a carpeted kitchen floor can be easy to maintain, especially if you choose a neutral color in a middle-range value or a cleverly camouflaging pattern. For easy cleaning, choose a synthetic fiber with a short, closed loop and soil-releasing backing. Commercial carpeting generally excels in these qualities. Do not use carpeting in a kitchen with a restaurant range or any other source of high heat, however.

Harder surfaces will not win the resiliency contest, being less cushy for the feet, but they are more immune to the effects of common kitchen calamities. Even an overturned tureen filled with borscht cannot mar the glory of these floors. Families with young children and pets often favor some form of vinyl or rubber surface, which also reduces noise.

Hardwood flooring is a good compromise between resilient and hard surfaces, especially when it is installed over a crawl space instead of on a concrete pad. Properly sealed with moisture-curing urethane, a wood floor has the low-maintenance virtues of carpet or vinyl sheet goods, and hardwood is undeniably handsome.

Other hard flooring surfaces are ceramic floor tile, brick, stone, slate, concrete tile, travertine, and terrazzo. These materials do not offer much resilience or sound absorption; they do offer durability, easy maintenance, and a very pleasing appearance.

The floor is the room's foundation, supporting all furnishings and other elements. As a general rule, the best color is a shade darker than that of the walls and ceiling so that the floor does not appear to float. On the other hand, a light floor reflects available light and gives

the kitchen a bright and open look. A subtle pattern and neutral color will contribute a feeling of spaciousness and free the attention for the room's other distinctions. A particularly eye-catching pattern on the floor will dominate the room—not a wise choice if other colors and strong design elements are planned.

The seam between floor covering and walls should be finished off with an appropriate trim. Wood floors are generally trimmed with wood baseboards, whereas ceramic tile may be finished with either matching tile (if the chosen style offers trim molding) or wood. The best finish for carpeting is wood trim, which may be coved (concave) in the toe-kicks. Vinyl sheet goods and tiles may be trimmed with wood, vinyl, or metal, also coved in the toe-kicks. For a brick, wood, or stone floor, wood trim is a best bet, but it should not be coved.

A skylight and stained glass window accent the interplay of ceiling heights and textures that lends excitement and drama to this kitchen.

Overhead Effects

• *How does the ceiling influence the character of a kitchen?*

The standard height of a ceiling is 8 feet. Any variation on that standard height will affect the feeling of a room. A kitchen with a lower ceiling may automatically seem cozy, intimate, informal, enclosing, whereas a kitchen with a higher ceiling will usually seem airy, expansive, formal, and dignified. A ceiling with multiple heights adds vigor to the space while subtly differentiating the cooking area from an adjoining eating or living area. Sloped ceilings emphasize the dimension running in the direction of the slope while calling attention to the highest part of the room. A single-slope shed ceiling sets an informal tone and has fine acoustics. A gabled or double-pitched ceiling increases the apparent volume of space. Large exposed beams overhead contribute drama, emphasizing the room's height. A coved ceiling offers the elegant grace of walls and ceiling curving into one another. For added natural light, volume, and even warmth, skylights have become a popular ceiling feature.

In addition to such structural effects, surface treatments include the usual paint and/or wallpaper chosen to coordinate with the rest of the decor. A light ceiling color will reflect light, creating an open and airy feeling, whereas a dark, subtle shade will cause the ceiling to seem lower and the room to seem more intimate. At night, reflecting artificial light, the color of the ceiling will influence other colors in the room. A yellow ceiling will bring out the yellows, oranges, or yellow-greens in the room, for example, while putting a damper on

blues and violets. A smooth ceiling texture is currently the favorite in contemporary homes. Textured plaster, tile, wood, surface-mounted brick, or metal (such as patterned tin for a turn-of-the-century mood) also offer a rich field of decorating possibilities.

Capable Counters

• *Which countertop materials provide the best service and wear for all-around use?*

Like floors, countertops perform workhorse duty in a kitchen. The ideal is a surface that can withstand chopping, a hot pan set directly on it, and the usual spills while also looking beautiful and complementing the rest of the decor. No single surface has all these qualities, but with trade-offs you can come close to the ideal counter surface.

Laminated plastics have long been popular. Available in a great variety of finishes and colors, these surfaces are among the easiest to care for—splashes and most spills will not mar them. However, plastics are not

This dark ceiling tone, picked up in the tile design and window woodwork, contrasts with the walls and cabinetry.

Butcher block counters add welcome warmth to this quiet, polished color scheme.

Ceramic tile offers an enormous range of handsome effects and is a practical counter surface as well.

suitable as cutting surfaces, so pull-out boards or hardwood inserts are needed.

Butcher block and other hardwood counters provide a pleasing expanse of cutting surface for carving meat, slicing vegetables, and for many other food preparation activities. Wood counters add lovely warmth to the room's overall aesthetics, often a necessary counterbalance to the unadorned style of contemporary kitchens. Despite their rugged nature, wood surfaces do not remain unscathed by moisture and spills, however, and hot pans will leave scorch marks. It is often a good idea to confine hardwood counters to the food preparation area. And to protect their porous nature, be sure hardwood counters are sealed with linseed oil or a varathene or varnish finish. Even with a protective seal, though, expect the surface to show food stains and knife marks.

Ceramic tile is popular, durable, and easy to main-tain. The tiles themselves are scratchproof, unaffected by spills, wipe clean in an instant, and can take the heat of pots coming off the stove. The trouble with tile is that the grouting, a porous material, does stain and is difficult to clean, although with recent improvements in grouting, this problem has diminished.

Not all tiles have smooth, even surfaces, either. For an effective countertop, ceramic tiles should be flat, square, and form an even surface so that your fragile crystal stemware stands steady on it. Uneven tiles should be restricted to vertical surfaces. Ceramic tiles offer almost unlimited decorating possibilities, with solid colors ranging over the color spectrum and hand-painted designs straight from native artisans from around the world.

Marble and granite are the preferred but expensive choices of bakers and pastry chefs. Their cool, smooth surfaces are ideal for rolling out dough or making candy. Marble is much more porous and difficult to care for than granite or synthetic marble such as Corian. These surfaces give a very rich and elegant look, although they are often used only in the baking area, not throughout the kitchen.

Corian, a synthetic marble, is an attractive and practical material for counter surfaces. It can be sawed, sanded, and shaped into pleasing finish details in a way that is not possible with natural marble.

Finally, stainless steel or metals such as brass or copper can be used, with dramatic and beautiful effects. Stainless steel is the most practical of these options, although it, too, shows surface scratches and even water stains. Brass and copper, generally for show, are rarely used, although now they can be treated with lacquer to protect them from tarnishing. It is best to place a glass sheet over them for protection.

The granite counters featured here establish a tone of elegance and sophistication while providing an ideal surface for pastry and candy making.

Throwing the Switches

• *What constitutes an effective lighting arrangement?*

Lighting is discussed last in this chapter, but it is certainly not last among kitchen design priorities. Not many years ago, one overhead fixture was used to light the entire kitchen. Not so today. Now it is known that proper lighting significantly reduces eyestrain and general fatigue. Like other elements of kitchen design, lighting serves both functional and aesthetic purposes. It prevents accidents and protects your health while setting a subtle mood and enhancing the decor.

A basic lighting plan calls for general illumination provided by a central overhead fixture, track lights, or recessed canisters; spot illumination over sink, cooktop, island, or peninsula; undercabinet lighting to illuminate counter surfaces; and usually a dropped fixture over the eating area.

With a separate control for each separate system, the amount of light in each location can be regulated. The general lighting system should have a switch at each entryway so that you can turn the lights on and off when entering and leaving, avoiding the hazards of groping your way across a dark room.

For general illumination, surface-mounted fixtures provide down-lighting and lateral lighting. Canisters recessed in the ceiling are also a good source of down-lighting for general illumination when carefully positioned so that light shines in an evenly distributed pattern. Track lights offer the greatest flexibility because the canisters can be aimed in any direction and the direction can be changed if the need arises; track lights are appropriate in contemporary-style kitchens. Although too large a number of canisters is required for general lighting purposes, track lights are excellent for lighting specific work areas.

Properly installed undercabinet light fixtures brighten the space below while the fixtures remain hidden and out of the way. A separate wall switch or a

Function and aesthetics combine in the lighting plan for this kitchen. Indirect fixtures accent the architectural features overhead, lending drama and a sense of spaciousness, while direct lighting—both stationary and pivoting—illuminates the work centers.

This sophisticated ceiling fixture evenly illuminates the room.

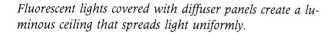

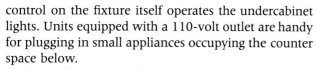

Fluorescent lights covered with diffuser panels create a luminous ceiling that spreads light uniformly.

control on the fixture itself operates the undercabinet lights. Units equipped with a 110-volt outlet are handy for plugging in small appliances occupying the counter space below.

Spot illumination over the cooktop is usually concealed in the range hood. Such units must withstand heat and moisture wafting through the exhaust system.

Just as light/dark aspects of the room should guide your color scheme, so they should dictate your lighting arrangement. Variations of the basic lighting plan may be appropriate depending on the amount of light needed because of the architecture of your kitchen, on the colors you have chosen, and on the amount of natural light that comes into the kitchen. A kitchen that gets little natural light during the day may benefit from a lumi-

nous ceiling—that is, fluorescent fixtures overhead behind diffuser panels that spread the light. Ceiling light panels usually need to be augmented by undercabinet and work center lighting.

Lighting can also contribute a sense of drama. Use indirect lighting to create a mood, a backdrop, or a feeling of spaciousness. A dimmer switch on the indirect system will allow you to vary the effect according to your mood or the occasion. And don't let your kitchen treasures languish in darkness. Put a spotlight on the display of heirloom crystal stemware; use down-lighting on the boxes of flowering plants at the windows; set a country mood with a floodlight on the hanging quilt. Lighting is the devoted assistant to every successful decorative effect.

CHAPTER 2

Preplanning

This kitchen layout was designed for practicality and convenience. Continuous counters connect the work centers in an uninterrupted flow, while the handy chopping-block island routes traffic away from the preparation area.

Before beginning plans for a new or remodeled kitchen, take an inventory of your present kitchen, assessing its weaknesses, its strengths, and its special needs. This preliminary scrutiny will help to translate vague feelings of dissatisfaction into a precise agenda for developing a greatly improved kitchen. The suggestions in this chapter will aid you in clarifying not only your needs and ideals, but also the nitty-gritty details of the job, namely, the length and scope of the work to be done, the financial commitment involved, and your role vis-à-vis building tradesmen and design consultants. A thoughtful assessment of these issues will lay a solid groundwork for coping with the job and handling any surprising twists in the road ahead.

Sizing Up a Kitchen's Efficiency

- *What questions should be considered in evaluating a kitchen's efficiency?*

A good place to begin is with your basic, spontaneous, heart-felt reactions to the room. Spend at least a week paying attention to your feelings and keeping notes. For example:

Assets

1. The exposed ceiling and beams
2. The view of the lily pond from the window at the sink
3. The walk-in larder with temperature-controlled wine storage.

Liabilities

1. Not enough natural light
2. Children always underfoot, invading my workplace
3. Isolation from guests when entertaining; no space for them to keep me company

Entertaining is an E.Q. (efficiency quotient) test of a kitchen's limitations, divulging flaws that don't come to light under normal use. Do guests cluster in an adjoining room exchanging lively talk just out of earshot?

Or do they sabotage the soufflé and your equilibrium as they swarm into the cooking area to check on the progress of the meal and raid the hot hors d'oeuvres? Perhaps you would like to put them to work on the romaine and celery, but the one sink is already occupied with dirty mixing bowls and roasting pan, and there is not a single free centimeter of counter space. Plan to entertain at least once during your survey week, keeping careful track of kitchen deficiencies. Notes of this sort can become the basis for a list of needed elements and attributes in the new kitchen.

To develop a thorough inventory of your kitchen's faults and virtues, take a hard look at the following specific areas.

1. Layout—Does your work triangle "work," or do you wear yourself thin traveling between work centers? Does the layout encourage through-traffic to bypass or trespass your territory? Do you have enough counter surface in crucial locations—next to the refrigerator, sink, and cooktop? Does the layout allow guests or family members to keep you company or to participate in meal preparation without impeding progress?

2. Storage—Are cabinets conveniently accessible to work centers, or do you traipse needlessly to and fro fetching tools and ingredients from one work center to another? Are drawers organized for finding items quickly and easily or does the vegetable peeler always disappear in an undifferentiated heap of utensils? Is crucial storage space taken up with useless odds and ends or with items that could be kept in some other part of the house? Do cabinets accommodate oversized equipment such as the electric mixer, the 20-quart stockpot and clam steamer, big serving trays, and so on? Do miscellaneous items constantly invade counters for want of proper storage?

3. Appliances—How do your appliances measure up to your family and entertaining needs? Are the refrigerator and range oversized for the space? Could you manage just as well with more compact, consolidated units that would liberate space for work surface and storage? Or does your culinary style dictate the opposite direction—multiple cooktops, commercial equipment, separate built-in ovens, a separate freezer?

4. Special work stations—Do family proclivities suggest the addition of a baking center with marble or granite surfaces and ovens near at head? Or a barbecue center equipped with an indoor grill, plenty of cutting surfaces, and storage for various barbecue implements? Do food preparation and cleanup activities compete at the sink? Do you need to incorporate a separate cleanup station or salad preparation station to keep the two

Two can work comfortably in this medium-sized kitchen, thanks to an auxiliary work station consisting of a commercial hot top with pull-out boards for added work space.

functions from tangling? Are you a multichef family, requiring tandem work centers?

5. Height considerations—For very tall people, the standard counter height of 36 inches is simply too low for working comfortably. Junior chefs often experience the opposite problem—the counter may be too high for them to reach. If someone in the family uses a wheelchair or has some partial physical disability, this also needs to be taken into account. Without altering all of the dimensions of your kitchen, some special counter-top adaptations can make the kitchen usable for all of your family.

6. Maintenance—Are the counters, floors, walls, and cabinets easy to keep clean? Do little footprints of children and pets suggest a different type of floor covering? Does your floor covering add to or reduce fatigue?

7. Lighting—Does your kitchen get enough natural light? Are windows positioned to give you a beautiful view? Should windows be expanded, moved, or added? Does the artificial light brighten each counter and work area while providing good general illumination?

8. Extra functions—Do you need to incorporate an eating area? A home office/computer center? An informal family gathering area with television and/or hi-fi components? A game room? A greenhouse for plants?

Setting the Style

• *How do you identify the aesthetic elements that are right for you and for your home?*

For some people, the answer to this question is quite clear. Perhaps you once fell in love with the lower Rhone valley; therefore, your kitchen must speak daily of those memories embedded in provençal pottery, lace curtains, and French country tiles. Or, your Victorian house will brook no compromises on authenticity—the kitchen must have period treatment.

Sliding mullioned windows open to the patio and pool area. The outside counter facilitates serving guests at poolside gatherings.

For most people, however, the array of choices can seem bewildering. The road to clarity begins with re-search in home-decorating magazines, books, and cat-alogues. Start clipping photos of appealing features, keeping notes of what you particularly like and why. This includes details such as hardware, moldings, and window treatments, as well as basic materials—counter surfaces, floor coverings, wall and ceiling treatments. This research will help to familiarize you with available decorating materials and ideas. And, after keeping at it for a time, your own taste will emerge and develop, and your preferences will become clear, along with some effective ways of executing those preferences. In work-ing with a designer, contractor, or subcontractors, a picture file will also be an effective means of commu-nicating exactly what you want and avoiding expensive misunderstandings.

In choosing the style of the new kitchen, take the room's existing architectural features into account. A high, coved ceiling tends to set a formal tone, whereas exposed beams and brick walls suggest an informal style. Certain structural elements may be too costly to move. Overhead ductwork, for example, can often be attrac-tively concealed inside false beams. Or, taking a neo-modern approach, overhead ducts can be painted and left exposed as a design element.

Finally, based on research and an emerging sense of the room's mood and style, there may be architectural or structural features that can be added. For example, you may want to incorporate a big stone fireplace to complement the massive beamwork overhead and to further the inherent rustic mood. French doors and windows can be installed, and cabinets can have mul-lioned doors. Possibilities may include a bay window, solar room, or skylight to bring in the natural beauty of the outdoors.

Who's Who in the Building Trades

• *Who actually plans and executes the design for a kitchen remodel?*

Kitchen remodeling is not an easy, do-it-yourself job unless plans are extremely limited—say, changing the floor covering or adding a fresh coat of paint and chic new window treatments. For changes on a larger scale, the average person will need help. To whom do you turn? For expertise in developing a plan that in-tegrates beauty and function, explore the services of an interior designer, architect, or kitchen designer. A kitchen designer specializes in the design of kitchens. An ar-chitect plans the design of the interior space, taking responsibility for any structural considerations and maintaining the period and design of the house. If plans include any sort of structural work—e.g., removing a bearing wall, adding a loft or a solar room—an architect should be consulted to ensure a good job and avoid costly, if not disastrous, mistakes.

Professional designers can work in varying capac-ities: simply planning the layout of cabinets, drawing up blueprints for the new kitchen, or actually coordi-nating plans and materials with the contractor who brings the plans to fruition. Fees, of course, will depend on the designer's level of involvement. The best way to find a good designer is through the recommendation of friends whose kitchens you have always admired. If you are considering someone without personal referral, give thoughtful attention to the individual's portfolio; ask

This kitchen required a period treatment suitable to the 1920s style of the house. The existing range from that era was retained, and cabinetry was fashioned to complement its style.

This old copper oven, which emerged as the walls were being stripped, was polished back to a patina and now adds visual interest to the remodeled kitchen.

A Dutch door adds a suitably old-fashioned touch to this warm-hearted country kitchen.

A mood of artful animation emerges from the careful coordination of palette with lively decorative tiles and display pieces to create a cheering though functional setting.

for and check references, establishing the extent of the person's role on any given job and determining his or her professional reputation.

A general contractor is the person responsible for executing the plans to specification. This includes hiring, scheduling, and supervising subcontractors, obtaining the necessary permits (not always, but usually), and ensuring that the work complies with building codes. To a limited extent, a general contractor may also offer basic design services.

Subcontractors are licensed for one area of specialty. They include the demolition crew, rough carpenter for framing, finish carpenter for finish details, cabinetmaker for custom cabinetry or cabinet installer for modular units, tile installer, plumbing contractor, electrician, floor covering installer (the trade depends on the type of covering), painter, and wallpaper hanger. If you are hiring and supervising the subcontractors yourself, make certain that they are licensed, bonded, and insured against any injuries that may occur on the job. Check their references for assurance that they will show up and perform their work competently. Be forewarned that coordinating the work of various subcontractors can be like choreographing a ballet. It is not uncommon to wind up with a chorus of tradesmen each blaming the other for the fact that the job has fallen behind schedule.

Work Flow Overview

• *What, exactly, is the sequence of events from plan to completion, and how long does it take?*

The answer to this question depends, of course, on the scope of the work. On a major remodeling, once you have finalized your design and "pulled" the requisite permits, as they say in the trade, the physical work begins with demolition—removing interior walls to consolidate rooms, tearing out cabinets and appliances you plan to discard, breaking through the ceiling to expose the roof—in other words, wrecking the kitchen before renewing it.

The first step on the road from rubble heap to *pièce de résistance* begins with framing in the structural mod-

ifications and additions such as the new French doors or sliding doors leading to the patio, or the extension of the sink window down to counter level, or the fulllength bay window replacing a solid wall. At this point, any new electrical and plumbing lines are installed for recessed lighting canisters in the ceiling, undercabinet lighting, the extra sink and dishwasher planned for the island, etc. Once the rough plumbing and electrical work are in place, the exterior walls are lined with insulation material, and then the plaster or wallboard goes up.

It is usually at this point that new cabinetry is installed, stained, and finished, followed by installation of countertops over the base cabinets. Next, the range, refrigerator, cooktop, ovens, dishwasher, and other appliances are hooked up to plumbing and electrical wires, cables, or conduit. Electrical lines also get connected to switches, sockets, and fixtures at this point, and all finish electrical and plumbing work is completed. Then the finish carpenter arrives to add moldings, hardware, and any other special detailing before the painter shows up to lay down a few coats of paint and brush out the woodwork before the wallpaper hanger installs the wall covering. As the final event, the floor covering—whatever material—goes down.

The length of time required for any remodeling, even minor, always seems to be more, never less, than what you imagine and agree upon with your contractor at the outset. This is a basic principle of the building trades, and there is always a very sound reason for delays. The tiles imported from Milan take 20 weeks instead of the usual 12 for delivery because of a work stoppage among Italian dock workers. Or, the major supplier of hardware has just gone out of business, causing a severe shortage of doorknobs all over town. For the sake of your equilibrium, work out a schedule with your contractor and then prepare for the job to take one-half to three-quarters longer. By all means, do not invite house guests or plan dinner parties until well after the scheduled deadline.

While most of the factors affecting the pace of completion are out of your control, there are a few things you can do to keep things moving along. *First*, order any custom-made materials well in advance of when they are needed. Keep track of the delivery schedule on all of your materials and keep after the suppliers if delays occur. *Second*, work out a week-by-week schedule with the contractor and keep an eye on all progress. Don't hesitate to question him if the work starts falling behind schedule. That is when the terrible tales of the Italian freight delays or of local suppliers suddenly going bankrupt will begin to reach your ears. Contractors generally respect clients who stay on top of matters. *Third,* do not change your mind unless absolutely necessary. Every equivocation, once construction has begun, adds time and money to the project.

Any remodeling that involves demolition of exterior walls can be scheduled during mild months only, from late spring to early fall. Unless you live in the sunbelt, where remodeling takes place throughout the year, be sure to take weather and climate into consideration when you plan the project.

Budgeting the Job

- *What general factors affect the cost?*

Cost, like schedule, depends on the scope of the undertaking. Yet there are several operations that will automatically shift the project into a higher price range. First, moving any structural elements such as bearing walls or rerouting plumbing or electrical wiring is expensive and constitutes major remodeling. Second, the quality of finish materials such as custom tiles, hardwood floors, and marble counter surfaces can also significantly add to the total costs.

A professional designer can help you specify complete plans and finish materials in advance so that their exact cost can be included in the contract you sign with the contractor. This is the surest route to an accurate bid. The contractor is then bound to provide the work and materials according to the signed agreement. If you do not specify finish materials in the contract, he will provide allowances—i.e., $5 per square foot for tile, $200 for hardware, etc. Rarely do the allowances allow for the quality of finish materials suitable for the job, and this is where budget surprises often appear.

These allowance surprises belong to a whole family of budget gremlins called "upcharges." These occur when the demolition crew tears down a seemingly harmless interior wall to find that it was harboring crucial ductwork that will now need rerouting at great added expense. Or, you might discover that the hardware specified is no longer available and the only alternative suitable for your handsome new cabinets is much more expensive. It is best to prepare yourself for such eventualities by allowing some percentage for upcharges.

If your budget does not allow for a full remodeling all at once, it is possible to upgrade your kitchen in stages. Following the general sequence of events described in the previous section, begin your first phase by replacing your old counters and installing the new sink, cooktop, ovens, or other appliances. Phase two entails facelifting the cabinetry: stripping and restaining the wood, changing the color, refacing the cabinets, accessorizing the interiors with customized racks and pull-out shelves, adding new hardware. Phase three includes wall covering and paint, and in phase four, installing the new floor or floor covering.

Upgrading in stages is not really feasible if your plan calls for a complete overhaul of the kitchen layout or if structural work is necessary. And, although the financial terms may be easier, the disruption to your life will seem endless. Even when you are between phases and your kitchen is functioning and usable, you will be haunted by the dissonances of old and new—spanking new appliances versus drab old cabinets—until the final phase is completed.

CHAPTER 3

The Small Kitchen

The dramatic angle of an open-beam ceiling bestows a surprising sense of spaciousness on this compact traditional kitchen. A tight U-shaped layout keeps every element within easy reach.

The small kitchen hardly requires an introduction. It is the place where culinary imagination and zeal languish in cramped quarters, often less than 120 square feet of space. It is a kitchen where family and guest assistance with meal preparation is a burden rather than a delight, where you routinely overturn the blender and its entire contents while bending to reach the cake pan. The small kitchen poses twin challenges to the remodeler's ingenuity: How can you gain crucial extra square feet of storage and countertop while simultaneously creating a feeling of spaciousness?

The Cosmetic Approach

Devices for Visual Deception

• *How can decorative techniques be used to relieve small-kitchen claustrophobia?*

As anyone who has ever been overweight knows, the actual dimensions of any physical body can be radically different from your perception of its size. You might say that the entire fashion industry is dedicated to visual illusion, mainly making people of all shapes and sizes look thinner. In a similar way, a few visual illusions from the decorator's bag of tricks can make a small room seem larger, open, and airy. This is where the traditional virtues of a light-hued palette play an effective role. Just as a dark suit can trim the dimensions of a body, dark shades will diminish the sense of space in a room. Those rich tones of chocolate or hunter green may deliver a dynamic designer punch, but in a small room you might begin to feel as though the walls are closing in on you. Light shades, by contrast, cause obtrusive cabinets and walls to retreat, to visually recede into the background. This visual strategy achieves its maximum effect when the color of the kitchen is unified with the color of adjacent or surrounding rooms. The harmony of color deemphasizes the actual boundaries of the kitchen and creates the impression of a much larger space, part of which is used for cooking. The eye-pleasing simplicity of classic white, off-white, almond, or gray has great popular appeal today because it embodies the merits of a monochromatic color scheme.

Despite the selling points of the neutral monochrome approach, however, you may not wish to adopt it, especially if your intention is to add warmth, spirit, or atmosphere to your kitchen. Use of color over a large expanse, such as an entire wall, can give a room a dramatic charge. In selecting the color scheme, consider choosing complementary colors for the walls and cabinets with a third, contrasting shade for accents. Many people have a reliable intuitive feel about color choice. If you don't belong in that category, be advised that colors convey specific emotional nuances. Bright red, for example, looks great on a Porsche 911, but in the kitchen will feel like an overdose of espresso and dominate the room. Hues of green, on the other hand, have a soothing effect, good for the person with a high-stress job or for a very active family. Any heavy, dark color, used extensively, can create a burrowlike atmosphere, to be avoided in a small kitchen. It is best also to avoid the patchwork effect of different colors here and there, a little of this, a little of that. To make a small kitchen beautiful, you must give careful consideration to all these factors.

Wall covering can contribute a feeling of spatial openness, but watch out for big, bold patterns that might dominate or overwhelm the room. Like light colors, small patterns have a recessive quality that pushes back

This classically simple color scheme offers warmth as well as an expanded sense of space.

A uniform light color treatment ties this small kitchen to the adjoining space, deemphasizing its size.

A daring contrast of rich colors adds excitement to this small kitchen. Track lighting and undercabinet fixtures show off stunning black plastic laminate counters.

A small-patterned wallpaper design on the ceiling continues down the walls to create a sense of spaciousness.

walls while remaining varied and interesting close up. A small-patterned wallpaper that matches or is a companion paper to the one used on walls can be used on the ceiling and any exposed wall space above the cabinets, with the visual effect of stretching the room upward. Better still is a ceiling treatment that continues down the walls to the level of the windows, guiding the eye to the larger vista of the outdoors.

Like intense paint colors, a spirited wallpaper can add a dash of personality to your small kitchen. Heeding the precautions about large patterns and mixed colors in a small room, do not give up entirely on dramatic wall coverings, even if you have a small kitchen. A large-patterned design can be used on one wall, on a section of wall, or on the ceiling, so long as the colors are analogous to those of the rest of the room. A vivacious wall covering will even establish the palette for the room, influencing the choice of other finish materials. In a small kitchen, it is especially important to coordinate door and window treatments with the wall covering to unify the look and avoid a patchwork effect. Matching window shades or curtains enhance the visual unity. Papering the doors (and their molding, if possible) will cause them to blend pleasingly into the walls. These suggestions are not appropriate for a large

design of contrasting colors, however, which if used at all should be restricted to small spaces such as the backsplash area. Used over a large surface, such a pattern would be too intense, dominating the room and detracting from everything else.

Judicious placement of mirrors can create the ultimate artful illusion. Completely covering one wall with mirrors will visually double the size of your kitchen or create a chimerical extra room. Positioned opposite your dining alcove, a mirror surface bestows both breathing space and an elegant reflection of a worthy table setting. A mirrored backsplash creates the impression of a pass-through from the kitchen into an adjacent room. And, in yet another application, beveled mirrors between the mullions on cabinet doors will multiply sparkling reflections, especially with polished copper cookware suspended opposite. Mirrors do show fingerprints, however, and if your family includes young children with a penchant for peanut butter and jelly, you might want to take that into account and place the mirrors beyond their reach.

Because of their clean and efficient lines, mirrored surfaces are most often seen in contemporary-style kitchens. However, if you have a traditional, country, or another style of kitchen, you can still use mirrors to

This wallpaper design delivers a touch of liveliness yet does
not overwhelm this small room. Green laminate cabinetry,
white counters, beige backsplash, and red accessories sustain the color scheme established by the wall covering.

Although actual floor space is limited, this open-beam, single-slope ceiling creates the effect of added space overhead, giving a liberated, unrestricted feeling to the room.

Box beams enclose lighting fixtures to add a sense of width to this otherwise narrow kitchen. Wallpaper extends from the ceiling down over the tops of cabinets to further the widening effect.

good effect. Simply choose framed and beveled pieces consistent with the style of your decor and place them to the best advantage as you would a work of art.

The ceiling also offers opportunities for perceptual deception. A mirrored ceiling above the dining area magnifies the actual height and the illumination when the dining fixture is turned on. And if you have a narrow galley or parallel type of kitchen, surface-mounted beams installed across the width will make the room seem wider. Of course, dark, massive beams crowded overhead will not bring about the desired effect with a standard 8-foot-high ceiling. Instead of large ones, use scaled-down beams for a small kitchen. Space them at equal intervals appropriate to the room. And stick to the monochromatic tones: natural wood finish against a light ceiling shade will achieve the greatest sense of expansiveness. In a kitchen with cabinetry running right up to the ceiling, beams may interfere with cabinet access, however. A handsome alternative is to install tongue-in-groove planks across the width of the ceiling.

For a contemporary or high-tech kitchen, a striking deviation from the light monochromatic color scheme is borrowed from the annals of retail store design, where overhead structural elements are left exposed, but skillfully disguised by a dark, matte finish color. The eye is drawn to the light shades on the surrounding walls, rather than to the dark area above. The ceiling, in effect, disappears. To work its magic, this ceiling treatment requires a vivid color contrast between the walls and the ceiling, with nonreflective matte finish overhead. A glossy finish would achieve the opposite and oppressive effect of drawing attention to the dark ceiling. This treatment also requires abundant natural and artificial light to compensate for the loss of light otherwise reflected from above.

Contrary to popular fear, you don't need a king's ransom to give your cabinets a touch of panache (though it helps). There are two pennyworth approaches to dealing with worn or outdated cabinetry. The first entails simply repairing unsightly woodwork scars with wood putty, followed by a conscientious sanding and a dashing new coat of paint, coordinated with tile and other decorative elements.

Or, if bulky, protruding overhead cabinets crowd your kitchen space, a surgical approach can lighten things up. Try removing the cabinet doors, leaving the shelves open to display your decorative pieces. If you do not want to have shelf contents exposed to the inevitable dust and grease, glass doors will protect and give an open appearance.

Another alternative is to reface outdated cabinets and add natty new doors. New doors and veneers can radically renew the look and style of your kitchen at a fraction of the cost of replacing all the cabinetry.

Portuguese counter tiles, new vinyl floor tiles, and fresh paint combined to create this sleek, attractive setting, which retains its existing layout.

Glass cabinet doors lend handsome detailing to the display of porcelain dinnerware. The transparent panels also open up the space to good advantage.

Small but Serviceable

• *Can cosmetic improvements offer low-cost options for maximizing efficiency in an awkward and restricted little kitchen?*

Upgrading the lighting system can make an enormous improvement in the functioning of a kitchen of any size. Appropriate lighting focused on work areas—countertops, the sink, the range—will drastically reduce eye strain and fatigue. Plan lighting based on the principles outlined in chapter one.

It is also possible to upgrade storage areas without getting into serious remodeling. The challenge here is to make every centimeter of space work effectively, especially the odd and inaccessible corners that often go unused. A trip to a builders' supply store will introduce an array of shelf and cabinet accessories designed to solve these problems. Cabinet doors can be fitted with racks that allow easy access to pot covers, aluminum foil and plastic wrap, herb and spice containers, and other items used frequently. Pull-out shelves in the base cabinets provide access to even the deepest recesses. Corner cupboards can be supplied with revolving trays so that no item is ever beyond reach. Adjustable shelves in overhead cabinets can provide maximum storage by cutting down on the otherwise unused space that exists between shelves.

Examine ways to consolidate functions in your kitchen. A countertop can often double as an eating area; peninsula arms can be designed to create work space, eating space, and storage. Use your imagination. If the various activities planned for a particular area are not apt to overlap at the same time, the multiple functions you project for it are probably feasible.

In coping with the small kitchen dilemma, common sense dictates that you scale down and streamline your furnishings and equipment. If possible, incorporate sleek lighting fixtures, flush window treatments, and recessed towel dispensers. Unfortunately, the small kitchen poses a great challenge to the packrat impulse. Clutter can be charming in a large country kitchen but insufferable in a small kitchen. Try to find new homes for all of those well-intentioned but ugly or useless housewarming and wedding presents that have pointlessly occupied valuable shelf space for years.

An existing cooler cabinet was fitted with easy-access storage shelves on the door; slatted shelves circulate air around perishable produce.

Even this small kitchen has a compact baking center, positioned between the cooktop and refrigerator. Baking spices tuck into a custom door rack, while baking equipment glides out of base cabinets on pull-out shelves.

An Emphasis on Form

This stunning showcase of contemporary design and efficiency started as a dingy little corridor kitchen with pantry. The transformation began with the removal of an interior wall between the kitchen and dining room. In its place, a handsome peninsula with cooktop defines the kitchen and lets the cook face guests in the dining area. A careful harmony of color, pattern, and line visually unifies the two spaces.

A pastel vaulted ceiling repeats the sculptural curve of peninsula and cabinets. Generous storage and food preparation counters occupy the wall to the left.

The central fixture warms the mood with a gentle glow of indirect light.

Echoing the curvilinear theme, custom-rounded oak molding lends panache to plastic laminate cabinets.

A king-sized mobile trash container wheels out from its corner housing to wherever it is needed. Its storage location makes skillful use of often-wasted corner space.

The peninsula houses a commercial cooktop suitably surrounded by an ample serving buffet. Luxurious black marble counters and backsplash add excitement to the subtle tones of pastel and light oak. Geometric ceramic floor tiles outline the kitchen area, establishing the transition from the hardwood floor of the dining area. Table service is ready at hand in peninsula cabinets facing the dining area.

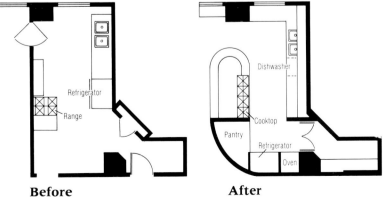

Before   **After**

Graced by a garden view, this peninsula functions as a snack bar, work surface, and pass-through counter for meals served in the dining area beyond.

Ideas for Minor Remodeling

• *Revamping the entire layout of a small kitchen—especially an older one—seems like the most effective way to get top value out of every inch and foot of space. With so many elements to consider, where does one begin?*

Start by consolidating your appliances as a first line of attack. Responding to the ubiquitous small-kitchen problem, appliance designers have produced some wonder-working, all-in-one models that perform nearly every function short of consuming the food for you. For example, there is a combination dishwasher/sink with built-in garbage disposer. Another unit performs three different functions: a dishwasher with a cooktop and an oven above that.

To accommodate double ovens, you might consider a bi-level range that has one oven beneath the cooktop,

one above. Or, if you want a microwave, there are models that come neatly stowed away in a cooktop ventilation hood. Another microwave model can be attached to the bottom of an overhead cabinet, hanging 9 or 10 inches above the counter surface. In both cases, your counter space is preserved. The glass or ceramic electric cooktops can also double as countertop when not in use for cooking.

Other space-saving options include a built-in refrigerator, with a standard depth of 24 inches, which is 6 to 8 inches less than that of a freestanding model. The small, under-the-counter refrigerators often used in bars, offices, and hotel rooms are yet another alternative. These refrigerators provide less than 10 cubic feet of cold food storage—not really practical for a family of four, but okay for keeping the milk and eggs from spoiling. For a narrow, one-wall, micro-sized kitchen, you can get a compact unit consisting of a range, refrigerator, oven, and sink all in one. This unit measures 5 feet long, and if you center it on your wall, you can construct counters on each side. Finally, if your kitchen has to double as a laundry room, look for a unit with

A micro-sized counter surface doubles as cooktop with Fasar cooking tiles.

washer on bottom, dryer on top. By replacing big, old, space-consuming appliances with lean, consolidated units, you will have much more room for storage, countertop, and other aspects of your kitchen.

Small Kitchen Layout Challenges

• *What considerations influence the arrangement of appliances and other elements of kitchen layout?*

First, as always, unless you are prepared for major plumbing expense, it is best to leave the sink right where it is and build your work triangle around it. In developing your plan, follow the basic guidelines outlined in chapter two, bearing in mind that the small kitchen presents special challenges in coordinating its practical function with its equally important social function. You may want to include subsidiary work stations where guests and family members can join in the cooking and cleanup without getting in each other's way. With space

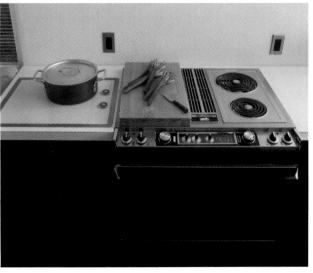

This versatile range and grill is fitted with butcher block and a glass induction cooking unit at left to extend the work surface, an element that is often at a premium in a small kitchen.

Angled cabinetry controls the traffic patterns in this long, narrow kitchen. Its contours allow two cooks to ply their talents at the same time.

Although limited in its floor space, this kitchen has a little desk against the end wall and cabinets. This bonus work space remains out of the way of kitchen activities.

gained by consolidating appliances, there may be room for a small banquette for eating, outfitted with a recessed television where friends can watch the ballgame while dinner is on the stove. Perhaps you would like a desk, tucked neatly behind the pantry cupboard, where menu planning, home computer activities, or homework/study can take place.

Another challenge in planning the layout of a small kitchen is organizing the flow of traffic so that it bypasses the work areas. Ideally, others should be able to move freely into and out of the kitchen, lingering for a chat or inspection of the evening meal, without getting in your way. If traffic flow creates a problem in the present layout, change the pattern by shifting the location of doors, which may also produce some extra counter and storage space.

Moving a door requires some minor structural work, cutting and framing the new door and plastering over the old one. A qualified carpenter can do the job; if electrical wiring is involved, the carpenter can tell you

Every refrigerator should have at least minimal landing space adjacent. In this case, a door was relocated in order to create counter surface next to the refrigerator.

The Conquest of Space

Inspired planning helped to transform a small kitchen's clumsy layout into a genial arrangement incorporating three clearly defined work stations. In the original layout, an awkwardly positioned door created a pattern of traffic right through the primary food preparation area. Shifting the door opening established a bypass while enlisting the old laundry corridor as a cleanup station. Eliminating a cramped yet space-consuming eating area also made room for a baking center framed by separate ovens and refrigerator.

The primary food preparation area makes the most of its compact space. The angled placement of the sink in the corner contributes needed extra inches of usable counter surface on either side. Open space above the left wall cabinets emphasizes the full width of the ceiling, adding to the spacious feeling created by the light monochromatic palette. A lazy Susan corner cabinet mobilizes the furthest recesses for storage.

A pull-out table for two provided a compact solution to the homeowner's desire for an eating area in the kitchen. When not in use for informal dining, it doubles as a handy extra work surface or disappears in a base cabinet. Glass doors on the wall cabinets contribute to the illusion of space in this narrow area.

Moving the doorway incorporated this underemployed laundry area into the main function of the kitchen. Stacking the washer and dryer provided space for the dishwasher, sink, and lots of storage. The new plan segregates the cleanup and food preparation areas, where the two functions once tangled. Undercabinet lighting throughout the kitchen beams down on each task area.

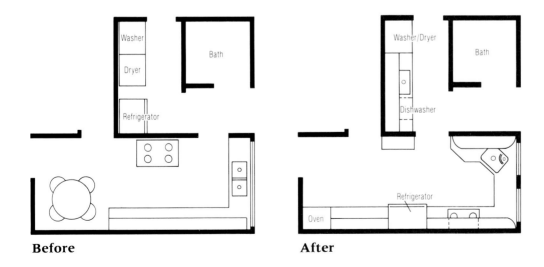

Before

After

Pocket doors of framed dowling separate the dining room from the kitchen while also unifying the two spaces. The two narrow pocket doors require smaller recesses in their respective walls than a standard-sized single door. The two-door style is a handy choice if pocket doors would otherwise intrude upon electrical wiring in the walls.

Matching treatments on this pocket door and surrounding wall create a unified field of wallpaper.

and you can call in an electrician to do the needed rewiring. If you decide to move a door or doors, there are many advantages to replacing a conventional hinged door with a pocket, or sliding, door that slides unobtrusively into the wall. Pocket doors eliminate the mayhem caused by doors swinging open in tight places, giving free access to cabinets and appliances. Pocket doors can be painted or covered to match the surrounding walls, which gives a unified look to the room when they are closed. When considering pocket doors, make certain that the recessed areas clear any electrical or plumbing fixtures.

Cabinets for Small Kitchens

• *What about replacing the old cabinetry?*

It goes without saying that cabinets often seem to dominate the kitchen. This effect can be minimized, however, by leaving 12 to 15 inches open between the tops of the wall cabinets and the ceiling. This narrow gap will add enormously to the perception of space without actually sacrificing storage room. The above-

This kitchen design, which dispenses with almost all overhead cabinets, is reinforced by a down-draft range, eliminating the need for a hood overhead. A glassed-in window extends the space into the living room while confining cooking odors and noise to the kitchen area. A windowed dining alcove takes advantage of outdoor beauty, adding extra light and a sense of dimension.

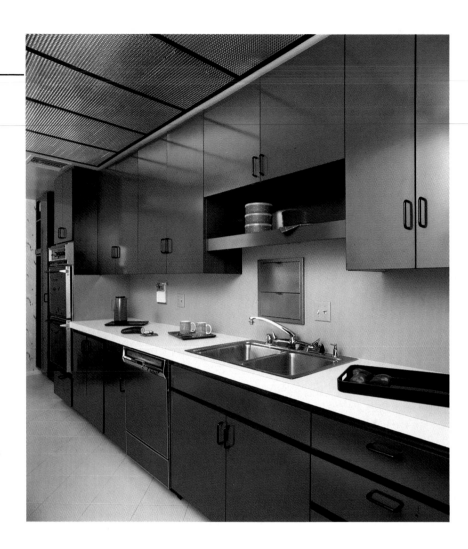

Cabinetry is restricted to the length of this small condominium kitchen, thus neatly dodging the problem of corner access on the return wall.

the-cabinet space is a prime location for display of large, attractive, and infrequently used serving pieces and other interesting items.

If you can do without them, eliminate the overhead cabinets altogether. This is especially effective for creating a sense of spaciousness in a narrow galley or corridor kitchen where overhead cabinets draw unpleasant attention to the room's cramped dimensions. Adding an overhead cabinet above a peninsula on the short end of such a kitchen will restore some of the lost storage space and help to balance the room's proportions. Likewise, tall cabinets positioned on the short return of an elongated kitchen will disguise the disproportionate length. Installing cabinets on only one wall instead of all along an L-shaped floor plan circumvents the obstinate problem of the corner cabinet's inaccessible recesses. If you do continue your cabinetry around a corner, be sure to outfit the corner cabinet with easy access devices such as lazy Susan shelves or half-round pull-outs, and leave a generous opening for retrieving and removing large items from the corner. In general, larger doors make it much easier to get items into and out of your cabinets. And, for a small kitchen, fewer doors and door handles streamline the appearance, as does the selection of lean, trim, compact units rather than heavy, hulking ones.

Finally, why not call in a carpenter to transform those odd-sized little spaces into extra custom storage for kitchen miscellany? If there is empty space behind a wall abutting the countertop—a broom closet, perhaps—a carpenter can create decorous little recessed hideaways for blenders, food processors, and other clutter. You might also consider recessing the cabinetry itself, which not only will prevent the cabinets from intruding visually but will gain you floor space as well.

To make the most of wall space between doors, cabinets and counters can be angled toward the doors to eliminate jutting corners and smooth the flow of traffic. And to extend counter space, have sturdy pull-out boards installed just above the drawers in base cabinets. In addition to their obvious merits, pull-out boards positioned lower than standard counter height provide the perfect work space for children or any members of your family who are confined to wheelchairs.

Customized treatment of odd-sized spaces maximizes the storage efficiency of a small kitchen where every inch counts. In this example, otherwise useless corner space is mobilized with the deft addition of angled drawer fronts.

A large utility closet furnishes a snug recess for the television.

Recessing cabinetry into an adjacent room supplies maximum clearance for this comfortable kitchen dining nook. Glass doors and open storage shelves in the cabinet add to a feeling of space in this modest corner.

A custom angled cabinet housing a commerical cooktop provides clearances around this bulky equipment. The cooktop's feet hide behind a hinged drawer front, giving the unit a built-in look.

Bringing in Sunlight

• *What contribution can a minor remodeling job make toward enhancing natural lighting?*

Remodeling offers additional opportunities for utilizing natural light by adding windows or enlarging existing ones. Extra windows can significantly reduce small-kitchen claustrophobia, creating the effect of extending the boundaries of the room. Though the kitchen itself is tiny, a window may extend the room right out to the apple orchard beyond the pool or all the way across the canyon.

Most kitchens have at least one window, usually located above the sink. This is a good place to increase the amount of natural light and the view from the room by extending that window right down to the level of the counter. The extra 10 to 15 inches of window can contribute immeasurably to the feeling of expansiveness. You might prefer, however, to install a greenhouse window. Models vary in price and require no special support system for installation. A north- or east-facing greenhouse window above the sink is a perfect location

for a home herb garden, which benefits from the moisture and steam produced in the sink. Moreover, if your window presents an unappealing view of your neighbor's laundry pole or dog run, you can fill the shelves of the greenhouse window with leafy plants that let in the light and provide an intimate, lovely garden to look at. When installing a greenhouse or bay window above the sink, avoid the common error of having the window beyond your reach. You should not have to climb onto the counter every time you want to open or wash it. To ensure a window within arm's reach, measure the width of the sink and allow 10 to 12 inches more—or whatever you find comfortable—for the window.

Another delightful possibility is a skylight, if the architecture of house and location of kitchen permit. A skylight gives you a little patch of infinity instead of a closed ceiling. If the kitchen has a northern or eastern exposure, in fact, a skylight may be the only way you can increase the amount of natural light coming into the room. Skylights come in standard units; nonetheless, it is best to have a professional handle the installation, to ensure that the skylight is fitted properly into

The glass roof on this bay window opens the overhead plane to the sky. Concealed track lights supply nighttime illumination.

the support system of the ceiling and that you get a proper seal on the unit.

In some cases, modifications might be required before a skylight can be installed. A steeply pitched roof can accommodate a skylight only by means of a well connecting the ceiling opening to the roof. The design

---

An expanse of window on a north wall brings a verdant view and natural light into what was once a small, dark kitchen. The overhead shelf conceals recessed lighting for the sink area and provides space for plants.

of the well will affect the amount and distribution of light coming into the room; a small skylight with a deep well will provide only a small spread of sunlight. To increase the spread, angle the walls of the well so that they are wider at the ceiling, narrower at the roof. In a kitchen with exposed beams, skylights can be installed between the rafters. This possibility, often overlooked, vastly enhances interior brightness.

A few precautions when planning greenhouse windows and skylights: be sure to get thermally treated glass to prevent heat loss. And, depending on their location, consider the possible need for awnings or louvered shades to control the amount of heat and light entering the kitchen.

A Complete Makeover

• *When undertaking an all-out overhaul, what are the possibilities for giving a small kitchen some medium-sized dimensions?*

The answer to this question depends, of course, on neighboring space—is there a service porch, spare broom closet, butler's pantry, laundry room, or breakfast room? Any underutilized adjacent spaces are prime candidates for structural consolidation.

Let's say you have a graceless little kitchen with a tiny laundry room at one end and a tiny breakfast room at the other. Because the space is so confining and unattractive, you find yourself using these rooms as necessity dictates, but with no real enjoyment or relish. For a proper breakfast, you retreat to the local diner. For dinner, the various offerings of the Chinese take-out menu often seem more appealing than trying to prepare a meal in your restricted little kitchen.

Through remodeling you can transform several small and unattractive rooms into one open, efficient, and cheerful room that beckons rather than repels you. After removing the walls that chopped up the space, laundry appliances can be stowed neatly in one continuous corner of the enlarged room. A cozy eating

A small, lackluster kitchen acquired both natural light and extra floor space when its ordinary sink window was enlarged into a generous bay window that encloses the sink.

This small but unobstructed space emerged from the consolidation of an existing kitchen and breakfast room. A beam marks the juncture and provides a transition from the squared kitchen ceiling to the coved ceiling beyond.

The High-Tech Aesthetic

The union of a small kitchen with its adjoining breakfast room set the stage for this pared-down neo-modern treatment. A briskly functional floor plan accommodates a full complement of commercial and residential equipment, enabling several people to work together efficiently in limited space. If a guest wanders in, he or she might be put to work mixing drinks at the beverage counter or chopping vegetables on the scaled-down island. Providing work stations for guests was, in fact, among this homeowner's criteria for the remodel.

The decor stresses functional simplicity, found in easy-to-clean laminate and stainless steel surfaces or the eye-catching air duct and comfortable rubber flooring. In the midst of such minimalism, the curved end of the island repeated in the wood-edged counter adds a graceful touch.

The new arrangement needed an intermediate work station to pull the floor plan together, yet the dimensions of the room could not support a full-sized island. The answer: an unusual 18-inch-wide island with counters extending over open shelves, perfectly scaled to the room's proportions. Eliminating the usual drawers and cabinets left passageways clear on all sides. The butcher block counter with marble insert suits many types of food preparation and features an opening with a dish underneath to catch crumbs, peelings, and liquids.

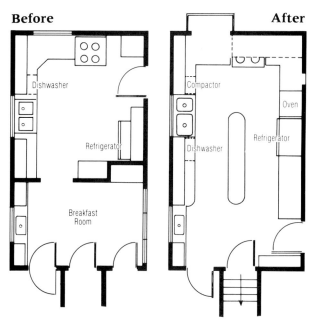

Before

After

A swinging steel restaurant door provides a whimsical touch, its shining surface complemented by utensils suspended from the exposed duct overhead. Homeowner's extensive cookbook library is located nearby for ready reference, while a small bar sink opposite comprises an auxiliary work station.

Tailored plug molding supplies electricity to small appliances. The commercial range sets the tone for a stainless steel backsplash and hood, which demarcate the cooking center. The abstract pattern of pot lid storage adds visual interest.

Extra-deep custom base cabinets mount flush with the commercial range. Full pull-out shelves provide handy storage for heavy cookware while maximizing the use of deep recesses: cabinet doors have been eliminated to open up the space. A greenhouse window integrates this slick, modern environment with the natural world, and fresh herbs flourishing in the window can get snipped and popped into a sauce or salad at a moment's notice.

Full-height cabinetry houses a spacious pantry, completely outfitted with pull-out shelves and conveniently located adjacent to the island and refrigerator.

nook can occupy the former breakfast room—demarcated by a functional peninsula work station or pass-through divider. Even the dining room or family room can be consolidated with the kitchen to provide a continuous flow of space, with the added benefit that the person working in the kitchen doesn't miss out on dinner conversation.

If consolidating interior space is not practical, consider adding a bay window alcove or even a sun room. These additions can be particularly successful if your kitchen adjoins an attractive patio or garden. Taking your morning beverage in a glass-enclosed sun room surrounded by primroses and morning glories can go a long way toward offsetting the stress of the day ahead.

The cleanup area is an excellent place for a bay window. Having the sink recessed in the bay leaves extra floor space, and the glass ceiling over the sink creates the pleasing effect of a limitless expanse overhead.

The structural work of removing walls and adding rooms is best left in the hands of a competent contractor, however, to ensure that a bearing wall does not inadvertently get demolished in the process.

CHAPTER 4

The Medium-Sized Kitchen

This medium-sized kitchen is not large enough for an island, so a rolling cart becomes a versatile way to extend work space.

The medium-sized kitchen offers a sizable field for the exercise of fantasy. Its spatial allowances—generally 120 to 170 square feet—are sufficient for expressing the unique architectural character of a home, capturing the beauty of landscape or garden, setting a mood, or reflecting the particular style of your family. Released from the tight reins of space restriction, the medium-sized kitchen offers greater possibilities for restyling the layout, such as adding a wall, island, or peninsula for efficiency and traffic control. The examples in this chapter are designed to spark the imagination, fueling it with some practical approaches to specific medium-sized kitchen problems.

Cosmetic Considerations

A Tasteful Medium?

• *How can light, color, and pattern be used to best advantage in a medium-sized kitchen?*

In a medium-sized kitchen, style is not limited by the challenge to overcome the inherent spatial problems posed by small and large kitchens. Consequently a sleek, chic high-tech look with pristine counters and lacquer-finish European-style cabinetry is as appropriate as a cozy Americana country style with an open hearth, exposed beams, colorful rag rugs, and early-American bric-a-brac decorating open shelves. The medium-sized kitchen can accommodate almost any choices you might make in response to the often bewildering question: "What do I want?" For a snug and open-hearted context for neighborly visits and family togetherness, look to warm hues—walnut, terra cotta, cocoa, maroon—with brass or copper accents and soft, indirect lighting. Bright primary colors, spirited patterns, contrasting shades, and direct lighting provide a cheerful setting for a vivacious family. Subdued but contrasting background tones marked by strong accents, geometric patterns, and cove lighting convey a mood of up-to-the-minute sophistication and savoir-faire.

Wall covering lends itself to a provocative variety of treatments in a medium-sized kitchen. Big, bold,

contrasting designs that easily overwhelm a small kitchen can give a medium-sized room a proper dash of conviviality. Likewise, a discreet pattern of analogous shades, which would tend to disappear in a large kitchen, can set a restful mood in a medium-sized room. The scale also allows greater flexibility in mixing related designs—say, a stripe and floral pattern on the walls with a companion floral-only design on the ceiling. Such a combination could easily seem fussy in a small room, but in a larger space it could pull the room together, unifying it through the continuity of color while providing a refreshing variety of pattern. If you choose a geometric pattern for the ceiling, you can echo the effect to good advantage in floor tile and countertop, picking up any subtle shadings in the grout. Clean and streamlined fixtures, cabinets, and other furnishings provide a fitting counterpart for a geometric theme.

An older home with high ceilings offers first-rate opportunities for visual play. The additional space overhead may allow for a subtly contrasting treatment of overhead cabinets and base cabinets—café au lait above with a dapper slate gray below. To further the effect, open up the corners of the base cabinets and continue the overhead tone in the cabinet interiors. An open corner cabinet is a perfect spot for an attractive vase or a piece of sculpture.

You might also try some evocative textural combinations—say, a wood or tile floor and beams as a visual foil for glossy-finish, plastic laminate cabinetry. Feel free to introduce brick, textured plaster, and other materials that would weigh too heavily in a small kitchen. Another approach is to vary the surfaces by adding marble or butcher block inserts to countertops or by setting off the counter surface with a contrasting material on the backsplash.

Dollarwise Storage-Stretching Options

• *What are the possibilities for maximizing storage capacity without overhauling the cabinetry?*

For kitchens of any size, the most budget-minded approach to storage efficiency is to outfit existing cabinets with an array of ready-made accessories available from a builders' supply store. Without calling in a carpenter, these devices can effect custom storage for pot lids, serving trays, cleaning products, and other sundry

A pleasing interplay of color, style, and mood lends distinction to this period kitchen. High ceilings, light fixtures, and cabinetry style express the original 1910s character of the house. Left unenclosed, the corner of a base cabinet becomes a genial display nook.

A gentle two-tone pastel palette sets a dignified mood in this example of period styling. Open shelf storage reveals a vertical groove pattern in the cabinet interior, which enhances this kitchen's distinctive look.

*Ultra-sleek contemporary styling reflects a simple elegance.
A solar room addition supplies bountiful sunlight while
recessed fixtures illuminate the area at night.*

*A simple cosmetic change can produce dramatic results. In
this kitchen the ceiling was covered with wallpaper and
the soffit painted to match, introducing a contrast that
gives the room its special vitality.*

items while also getting mileage out of your cabinet doors and otherwise impenetrable corners.

A medium-sized kitchen can also handle pieces on open display without producing a suffocating clutter. Wherever there are exposed walls, you can freely add narrow, 9-inch shelving to display plates or other collectibles or to keep cans or spice containers from straying. Even cookware can become a decorative element in the kitchen, suspended above the cooktop from a hanging pot rack or against the wall on pegboard or a wire grid. Any of these options frees storage space for other purposes.

Other kitchen accoutrements can yield some surprising storage opportunities and multipurpose functions. For the odd-sized space, what about a chopping-block table with storage shelves underneath? Or perhaps a rolling cart equipped with a chopping block or with drawers and shelves for storing your dinnerware? Keep it stowed out of the way between meals and roll it out for step-saving table setting and serving.

This trim base cabinet provides pull-out storage for casserole dishes and, in vented bins, for fresh fruits and vegetables.

A lazy Susan shelf tackles this problem corner, while the adjacent cabinet houses both a wire pull-out produce bin and shelf for the mixer.

With a cutting-board surface, this handy mobile cabinet can function as an auxiliary work counter wherever additional work space is needed.

Framing the walk-in pantry, narrow adjustable open shelves display a charming medley of favored objects.

Ideas for Minor Remodeling

Exploiting Your Kitchen's Assets

•   *What are some design ideas for enhancing a kitchen's strengths? Or turning liabilities into advantages?*

Remodeling a medium-sized kitchen often involves simply improving, emphasizing, and making the most of what is already there. Perhaps the kitchen needs some additional storage or work space or a more effective layout. A medium-sized kitchen is less apt to need the sort of sweeping changes required by its small and large counterparts. Analyze what is best about your medium kitchen and utilize it to the utmost.

If your home is situated in attractive natural surroundings, make certain that the kitchen takes full advantage by enlarging or adding windows to capture the view. Consider removing a wall, substituting a peninsula or pass-through to open up the kitchen to views through windows in a neighboring room.

You can also carry the outdoor motif into your decor—for example, use walnut cabinetry and jade-green tiles to suggest a pine forest. Or a Sante Fe palette with wood and copper accents to suggest the desert landscape at sundown. By continuing the motif in your other decor, you effectively blur the distinction between outside and inside while calling attention to the beauty of the natural setting. Or you can contrast your decor with the outside scene by using greenery as a backdrop for light, sandy colors.

Another approach is to work with the architectural character of a house, using hardware, drawer pulls, ceiling fixtures, color scheme, floor treatment, and textural qualities to express the particular period style. Let's

A full wall of windows, capitalizing on the garden vista, influenced the placement of the island, which was positioned so the cook could enjoy the view while working.

say your kitchen has exposed rough-hewn beams overhead. You could extend the feeling with brickwork—possibly a brick arch over the cooktop slyly concealing a ventilation hood—and an open fireplace. Depending on the configuration of your kitchen, the hearth can open in more than one direction, exposing both the cooking and eating areas to its warmth and comfort. Extending the theme to the woodwork, you might add a fireside bookcase to house your cookbooks and collectibles. You can also emphasize unusual architectural detailing in the windows and walls by eliminating overhead cabinets that compete for attention.

Ceiling treatment offers many alternatives for influencing the character of a kitchen. Opening up the ceiling to expose the beams or to create a vaulted effect establishes a feeling of spaciousness. If your ceiling construction prohibits such daring developments, the simple addition of a skylight, as prescribed in the previous chapter, can contribute enormously to the sense of ver-

This corner fireplace warms the kitchen with its crackling blaze. Built neatly into the cozy brick structure, a set of shelves displays a collection of cookbooks.

*Textured plaster and a large skylight with gleaming metal
accents combine to establish a bright, cheery Southwestern
modern look in what was once a dreary, outdated kitchen.*

*This medium-sized kitchen acquires a king-sized feeling
from the massive open-beamed ceiling system overhead.*

Overhead cabinets play an unusually limited role in this kitchen, where ceiling structure, window placement, and the Bauhaus-inspired architecture of the house itself were the paramount considerations in the design.

tical dimension and the abundance of natural light. Of course, the larger size of the kitchen allows you to have a larger-scale skylight. A larger skylight should be equipped with automatic vents to expel hot air during the summer months and louvered shades to control the amount of sunlight and heat that is channeled into the room.

Renovating the Storage

• *What is the best way to truly customize cabinetry?*

Tailoring storage to the special needs of your family and your work style can give enormous satisfaction and enable kitchen chores to go more smoothly. It is tiring, as well as frustrating, to grope and scrounge for misplaced items. Thoughtfully arranged storage goes a long

This ingenious skylight not only brings in the sun and fresh air through an electrically controlled vent but also furnishes convenient and attractive pot storage.

A trio of skylights casts a soft glow of natural light in this elegant contemporary kitchen; a companion trio of round windows gives the sink wall a dash of excitement.

way toward channeling your energies into the creative aspects of kitchen work instead of into tracking down tools and materials for cooking.

Begin with a critical evaluation of work centers and their specific storage needs. Organize your dinnerware, table linens, cookware, utensils, small appliances, dry and canned food staples, cleaning products, plastic containers, laundry supplies, pet food, trash containers, picnic basket, and any other miscellany into their respective work centers. Now assess which things can be stored for easy retrieval and which cannot.

If your kitchen appliances were inherited from a builder or from previous owners, assess their appropriateness for your needs and for the available space. Many kitchens, especially those in tract homes, are routinely outfitted with equipment that is oversized for the space. If this is the case in your kitchen, consider exchanging some or all appliances for more appropriately sized pieces or even some of the consolidated, space-saving units described in chapter three. This will free up additional space for cabinetry and other storage options. If you are keeping the existing cabinetry, a skilled carpenter or cabinetmaker can help you tackle the trouble spots. Installing pull-out shelves on glides in base cabinets is a good, basic place to begin. Whatever else your kitchen requires, pull-out shelves will ensure that you get the utmost out of the farthest reaches of your cabinets. To the same end, you might have half-round pull-out shelves installed in corner cabinets. Another effective measure is to build partitioned dividers in cabinets for separating long serving platters, trays, cookie sheets, baking pans, pot lids, and other such odds and ends. Special dividers in a drawer near your cooktop can accommodate spice containers so that they are handy and easy to identify. Drawer partitions lined with Pacific Cloth—a felt chemically treated to counteract tarnish— can offer a protective storage option for silver flatware.

A pull-out cabinet in the vicinity of the sink can be outfitted with bins for discreet handling of trash, perhaps including one bin for disposable trash and another for recyclable trash. Pull-out bins in base cabinets also provide excellent storage for unwieldy, economy-sized sacks of dog food. Vented bins in cabinet drawers are excellent for storing fresh vegetables.

For pantry items, install narrow can racks on the pantry door or transform a 24-inch-deep wall cabinet into a pull-out pantry with 12-inch shelves on each side of a central divider. If pantry space is at a premium, size up the utility closet to see if the brooms and dust pan could make room for a few pantry shelves.

If you are making sweeping changes in your cabinetry, you might as well also install generously sized 20-inch cabinet doors instead of the more common 12-inch ones. The larger doors give much better access to the contents of cabinets.

Finally, what about the blender, mixer, food processor, juicer, toaster, espresso machine, etc.? It is convenient to have such appliances out on the countertop, available for ready use. And yet, unless there is vast countertop space just yearning to be so occupied, these crucial amenities of modern living can easily cramp workspace, create clutter, and impede cleaning. A tidy solution to this ubiquitous problem is to create appliance "garages," cubbyholes for all your countertop machines. Such garages can be neatly recessed into an adjoining broom closet or built right onto the countertop. If added to the surface of an island or peninsula that separates the cooking area from the eating area, such hideaways have the salutary effect of shielding kitchen cleanup mess from the view of diners while providing a food-processing center. Another option for a mixer is to store it on a pop-up caddy in a base cabinet, preferably in the vicinity of your baking center. Most of these appliance storage options are also available in prefabricated modular units or in custom cabinets ordered from a cabinetmaker. If your choice is to purge the entire lot and bring in new cabinetry, be sure to analyze and specify the custom features suitable for small-appliance storage.

If cubbyholes and custom cabinetry do not solve storage problems, another expedient is to recruit any available closet or cabinet space in an adjacent room for auxiliary kitchen storage.

Mobilizing Work Space

• *How can extra counter space be chiseled out of a medium-sized kitchen?*

Often in a small or medium-sized kitchen, extra work space can be acquired only through the sacrifice of storage space or some other useful feature. In devising more efficient work space, the bottom line is establishing your priorities: what do you need and where do you want it?

If work space is your kitchen's Achilles' heel, tackle the problem first by establishing proper storage, following the guidelines in the previous section. Here, espe-

Half-round base cabinet shelves reach back into corner recesses to bring bowls and cookware front and center.

Pie tins, cake pans, and pot lids fall into tidy compartments in this deep partitioned drawer.

Spices retain their freshness in this cool, dark drawer located in handy proximity to the cooktop.

A Pacific Cloth lining protects the patina of silver stored in this partitioned silverware drawer.

A recess between the wall studs houses spices for the cooking center.

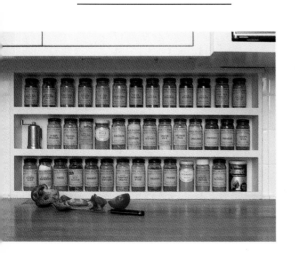

Designed with a concern for easy physical maneuvering, this full-height cabinet features partitioned tray storage above, pull-out shelves for table linens below, and storage for heavy items in the mid-range, where they can be lifted with the least strain.

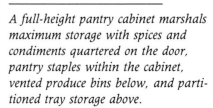

A full-height pantry cabinet marshals maximum storage with spices and condiments quartered on the door, pantry staples within the cabinet, vented produce bins below, and partitioned tray storage above.

Mixer is attached to handy pop-up shelf for convenient use and storage in this baking center.

Twin trash containers in a pull-out drawer allow for segregating recyclable trash from common refuse.

Small appliances are readily accessible in this corner "garage."

These knives are stored right where they are needed, inserted into custom-made slots in the countertop. The submerged blades fit safely behind pull-out shelves in the base cabinet.

An island baking center is doubly efficient thanks to a handy storage nook that shelters the blender and food processor (with blades stored in individual slots).

cially, recessed storage may be the answer. A recessed row of spice shelves can fit nicely in the wall between studs, keeping the counter surface free. A portable microwave unit, often a demanding occupant of counter surface, can be built into an overhead cabinet or in the base cabinet below, leaving plenty of head space for the individual working at the counter.

If you need still more work surface, is there a door that could be closed off to give a continuous counter surface and also divert traffic from your work space? Another practical solution is to have a cabinetmaker install pull-out boards, where possible, in base cabinets to extend counter space. If you cannot afford to lose the drawer storage, have butcher block or hardwood

inserts cut to fit the tops of your drawer frames. The drawer remains a drawer but, with the removable insert added, it doubles as a work surface. Such lower work surfaces are just right for children who enjoy pitching in and also for someone confined to a wheelchair. Some furniture options—a chopping block table, roll-away cart, or even the breakfast table—can often add the extra work surface needed when Thanksgiving guests offer to help with meal preparation.

Another very effective solution to the work space dilemma is to add an island, if the width of your kitchen permits (remember: you need at least 42 inches clearance on each side) or a peninsula or island in place of the wall separating the kitchen from the breakfast nook

Table linen, flatware, and glass storage in this peninsula opens out toward the dining area.

A new pass-through links the butler's pantry with the cooking area in this gracious traditional kitchen. The kitchen counter was designed to conform to the height of the existing counter in the butler's pantry.

A pull-out board stretches the work space in this bake center, which is equipped with a marble counter insert, a second sink (positioned in the corner to maximize usable counter space), and generous undercabinet lighting.

or dining room. Islands and peninsulas provide fitting accommodation for the extra cooks that occasionally populate one's kitchen, while also greatly expanding storage capacity. If an island or peninsula demarcates an eating area, it is a good idea to plan access to storage from both sides, keeping the table service in convenient proximity to the dining table. A pass-through, another expedient option, offers the convenience of a counter accessible from both sides of the wall.

Of course, if working with the existing space still does not take care of your needs, then it is probably time to consider a major remodeling.

Giving It the Works

• *How do you go about planning a major remodeling?*

In any type of remodeling, the first item on the agenda is to analyze exactly what you want and need. A large-scale remodeling effort adds to the possibilities available for creating the kitchen of your dreams.

If kitchen space is too limited for the needs of your family, consider the ideas described in chapter three for consolidating interior rooms. You may also want to consider adding on to your home, or converting another room into the kitchen (such as a den, bedroom, or dining room), or moving a wall back into a neighboring room. You may decide to remove a wall and join two rooms for one continuous space, incorporating other functions, such as a planning center with desk and file cabinets. If the adjacent outdoor space permits, a sun room or greenhouse addition can effectively bring out-door attractions right into the kitchen, along with a cheery abundance of natural light. The addition of a sun room can balance the sometimes disagreeable proportions of a narrow kitchen. It can also provide the clearance you need to incorporate other elements, such as a peninsula or an island.

A top-to-bottom overhaul offers tantalizing opportunities for transforming a run-of-the-mill kitchen into a pleasing environment that uniquely expresses your personality and serves you well. It allows you the satisfaction of adding the sort of personal touches that are not usually possible with minor remodeling. Occasionally, for instance, as a result of consolidating rooms, the new ceiling has different angles and varying heights. Resurfacing the ceiling to emphasize differences in overhead angles becomes a dramatic design feature that can influence the layout and the decor. In a similar way, a major structural element such as a steel supporting beam can contribute to a kitchen's distinc-

tion if you treat the beam as a design element, using a striking paint or other surface treatment to lend drama to the decor.

A major remodel is an opportunity to bring the elements of a kitchen into harmonious alignment with one another, creating a distinctive look and style. It gives license to a thoroughgoing coordination of the decorative touches—say, pewter and white checkerboard vinyl tiles on the floor, accented by polished steel drawer pulls, a stainless steel sink and faucet, and a hanging chrome pot rack.

If the kitchen is connected to a surrounding room by a pass-through or peninsula, giving both rooms a unified treatment will deceive the eye and make the two spaces seem like one large space.

A major remodel also enables—even requires—you to rethink your appliance needs more thoroughly. Angling the sink in a corner, for example, will give more usable counter and work space on each side. If you then install a dishwasher and trash compactor, each

To accommodate an eating area, a solar room was added. An automatic temperature control opens vents to discharge hot air.

An Illusion of Space

A modest one-story house is the setting for this striking contemporary kitchen. Originally a bedroom, the space was converted for kitchen duty because the homeowner needed a dining room, and it was determined that the existing kitchen was not suited to extensive remodeling. The old kitchen subsequently became the dining room, and the adjacent bedroom developed into the new, larger kitchen pictured here.

The transformation from bedroom to kitchen was not just a matter of installing plumbing, cabinets, and appliances and then setting up shop, however. The room originally had a ceiling of two different heights, 7 and 8 feet, which made for an awkward, unwieldy space. Furthermore, space was still limited, so careful planning was necessary to create a functional, aesthetically pleasing kitchen.

The finished room has three distinct work areas—for food preparation, cleanup, and baking. Its new irregular 20-foot ceiling creates a sense of expansiveness and provides an interplay of angles, light, and surfaces.

Structural elements combine to form the backdrop for a host of amenities, such as the sink, which was placed in the corner to take advantage of the view out the windows, and the butcher block island, which houses the cooktop and includes seating for food preparation and eating. Stainless steel-trimmed European laminated plastic cabinetry offers sleek styling.

Clean lines, effective use of space, and dynamic color scheme characterize the kitchen. The pole required to support the expanded ceiling becomes a design element when incorporated into the island.

Homeowner prepares fresh foods more often than frozen or canned, and opted for a full refrigerator and a separate undercounter freezer. This combination offers the advantage of extensive refrigeration and efficient, low-profile freezer space.

Because space is at a premium, a pantry is combined with a utility closet alongside the refrigerator.

Lighting can be a problem in a room with a high ceiling, but here track lighting on dimmer controls offers the necessary flexibility to illuminate the area effectively.

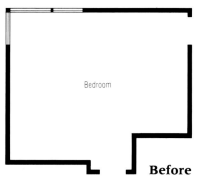

Bedroom

Before

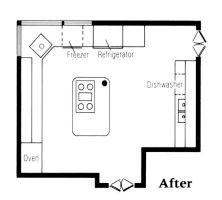

Freezer   Refrigerator

Dishwasher

Oven

After

Cleanup center is located adjacent to the dining room, so dishes from a dinner party travel only a short distance to the sink, dishwasher, and storage cabinets. Batwing doors open upward and stay well out of the way in an area where household traffic patterns are heavy.

A pull-out cutting board offers additional landing and work space in the cleanup area, a plus if several people are working in the kitchen at the same time.

Angling the counters and positioning the sink in the corner maximized work surface in this trim example of efficiency.

A striking paint treatment turned these supporting steel beams into a lively design accent.

one a cabinet's width away from the corner, the doors of both appliances can be open at the same time without interfering with the person standing at the sink. If you prefer a commercial cooktop (which has a greater depth than residential models), it can also be accommodated by placing it at an angle in a corner. In that position, it will not destroy the lines of your kitchen by jutting out from the counter.

Other popular appliance ideas include a warming drawer, which should be mounted flush with cabinetry,

within easy reach of the cooktop, and an undercabinet freezer, which can provide handy extra space without taking up the room required by a full-sized freezer.

A major remodel may involve adding space, converting space, or simply gutting the existing space and starting over. All these approaches require a careful look at layout options, as you will essentially be starting from scratch in planning your new kitchen. Unlike a minor remodel, you aren't apt to alter just a few aspects such as storage or appliances.

A large triple sink occupies an angled corner, with dishwasher and trash compactor positioned for easy loading. The overhead cabinet, at left, houses dishes and glassware.

Positioned at a convenient height, this useful warming drawer keeps food crisp or moist, as desired.

This commercial cooktop rests in a black-tile corner cavity, which prevents it from protruding into the room. Corner placement also frees counter space for other purposes.

Traffic and Layout Troubles

• *What can be done to remedy an inefficient layout?*

In a kitchen of any size, a well-planned layout achieves a smoothly functioning work triangle of storage, preparation, and cleanup, with properly proportioned amounts of counter space in between. (See chapter one for basic guidelines on clearances between the elements of the work triangle.) In a medium-sized kitchen, there are several alternatives for maximizing the efficiency of the layout. You can completely rearrange appliances and respective work centers to create a continuous flow of activities. You may also be able to close off or move doors that interrupt work surfaces or create disruptive traffic patterns. Another possibility is to remove an interior wall in order to create a continuous flow of space between the kitchen and an adjoining room. In this case, it is crucial—as mentioned—to coordinate the decorative elements of the two spaces. If space permits, you can also create secondary work

Removing the entry hall wall effectively joined this kitchen with the living area in a free-flowing open plan enhanced by the light palette and open shelf storage.

Careful coordination of line, texture, and color unifies the kitchen and living room. A rug defines the dining area while coordinating tone and texture with the living room.

Modern Efficiency, Victorian Detail

Echoes of the Victorian era set the tone for this alluring kitchen designed to combine cooking with informal entertaining. Revising the existing floor plan, which was interrupted by too many doors, posed the challenge of unifying the work centers while removing them from the flow of traffic to create a flow of space that would enable guests to wander in and serve themselves. An efficient U-shaped plan provided a workable foundation. Cleanup and table service storage are isolated on one arm of the U, out of the way of food preparation and cooking, which take place opposite. Refrigerator, ovens, and pantry are grouped against an interior wall to minimize their tall, bulky presence. A central island

Period charm and an efficient layout distinguish this modern Victorian-style kitchen. The marble surface of an island dining bar does double duty as a baking center, while the contrasting color scheme with gleaming brass accents creates a setting of sparkling distinction.

pulls it all together, positioned midway between the cooking and cleanup stations.

Consolidating the work centers around the east and north walls left a clear passageway along the west wall. French windows and doors along its entire length infused the interior space with natural light and outdoor scenery. Period lighting fixtures in concert with recessed and undercabinet lighting enhance the mood while furnishing ample general and task illumination. To complete the open plan, an adjacent breakfast room was created by removing an unnecessary staircase and separating the space from the work area by a peninsula. The trim banquette design of the eating area itself leaves extra space for a stereo cabinet and planning center with desk, files, and storage.

The Victorian theme is carried out in exquisite detailing. An elaborate border trim enhances the rich texture of the painted tin ceiling. Black glass appliance fronts complement the leaded glass cabinet doors and unify the look. Behind open shelves, mirrored surfaces reflect the sparkle of brass and glass. Marble counters maintain the Victorian ambience.

The Victorian decor is reflected in the texture of the painted tin backsplash, dark cabinets furnished with handsome leaded glass doors, and sleek marble counters.

French windows and doors brighten the interior with abundant light. Separate sinks segregate cleanup activities from food preparation while the central island integrates the work stations.

Embossed tin ceiling and a graceful transition of colors and textures establish the harmony between the kitchen and multipurpose eating area, which are defined by a peninsula.

A custom brass lighting fixture embellishes the decor while incorporating handy glass and cookware storage.

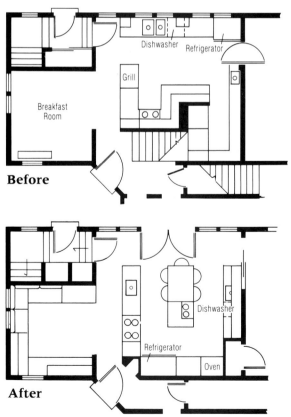

Before

After

The open plan for this kitchen was devised for a gourmet cook who likes to socialize with guests while seasoning the potage de poisson.

centers—perhaps isolate cleanup activities from primary food preparation. Again, your needs and desires will dictate which of these options will work best.

Even when radically rearranging a floor plan, it is usually best to plan around the present location of the sink. Stove, refrigerator, and cabinets can be relocated at a fraction of the cost of rerouting plumbing. Even if you are converting another room or adding on, the placement of the sink will probably be determined by existing plumbing lines; your kitchen designer, contractor, or plumber can help you locate plumbing.

Adding an island is a popular and effective means of unifying scattered work centers. If you can achieve sufficient clearance (adjusting the size of the island may do it), an island can be positioned smack in the middle of the kitchen to shorten distances between appliances and food preparation areas. An island can serve as a functional and stylish divider, distinguishing the kitchen from the dining area or the family room. It can accommodate a cooktop or range for the convenience of serving, or incorporate a snack counter. A ventilation hood overhead—styled to the decor of your kitchen—can reinforce the separation of the two areas. Or, if you wish to preserve a continuous flow of space between the kitchen and adjacent room, you also have the option

of installing a self-venting, down-draft range that requires no obstructing hood. Equipped with sink, dishwasher, and trash compactor, an island can also function as a handy cleanup station, ready to receive dirty dishes directly from the dining table. A trim set of shutters or sliding panel doors that pull down from above can hide the cleanup area from contented diners lingering over coffee. If your medium-sized kitchen is not quite spacious enough to accommodate an island comfortably, all of the same functions can be served by a peninsula, which takes less space.

In addition to their other functions, islands and peninsulas also perform a crucial role in traffic control, cleverly guiding large and small trespassers away from work space. An island counter with well-positioned stools keeps visitors out of the way while they keep you company. Of course, if others wish to put their shoulders to the kitchen wheel, they can enjoy the pleasures of industry at their very own island work station. You can further reinforce the traffic pattern by creating different floor heights—step up to the kitchen from the bypass route around the island.

If the island/peninsula solution is not appropriate for your kitchen's configuration, perhaps because of inadequate width, adding an interior wall in the crucial

This cooking island with dining bar pulls the three work centers into comfortable proximity.

An angled peninsula creates an efficient work area by guiding traffic to and from the solar room beyond.

Bi-level floors and a contoured island demarcate the kitchen from the traffic bypass route. Light oak floors lend a touch of warmth to the upper kitchen level; the lower-level passageway features ceramic tiles.

place can serve as a traffic guide. And once you have gained additional exposed wall space, you may want to use it for an extra work center or appliance or whatever your needs suggest.

Fashioning a Kitchen Café or Planning Center

• *With so many functions taking place in the kitchen, what are the possibilities for creating or keeping an eating area or a cubbyhole desk space?*

Many people feel that having a spot in the kitchen where you can sit down and grab a bite to eat is an essential of modern living—a casual setting for the cas-

The European Approach

Removing a single wall between kitchen and breakfast room enabled the tiny kitchen of a terrace apartment to evolve into this stylish remodel. But, as part of a multistory structure, the position of doors and windows was fixed, imposing limitations on the scope of the new design. Placement of windows dictated the arrangement of the cabinets on the window wall, and the location of the sink was determined by the existing plumbing. Rearranging appliances within the new, larger space produced a comfortable and efficient work area that takes full advantage of window views.

Chic European styling dignifies the decor with imported modular lacquer cabinetry, appliances, and accessories designed for aesthetic compatibility and uniform scale. A sharply contrasting color scheme highlighted by the high-gloss finish of the cabinetry enhances a mood of sophistication and drama.

A granite-surfaced peninsula graciously curves to accommodate seating and increased counter space while directing traffic flow within the highly functional work area. Cabinetry was installed along the perimeter of the ceiling to unify the room visually.

A streamlined wall of continuous cabinetry, its location retained from the original layout, offers a lustrous granite serving buffet that doubles as extra work surface, with an even bank of undercabinet lighting.

Beneath the peninsula counter, a temperature-controlled wine closet brings out the best in vintage grand cru.

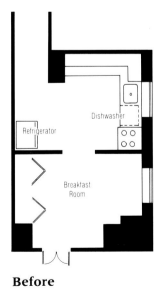

Before

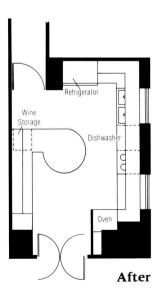

After

Smart European-made ovens occupy a nook on the return arm of the main work counter. The granite surface invites baking activities while providing landing space for spécialités de la maison emerging from the oven.

A lacquer ceiling fixture extends the decorative theme while concealing an indirect lighting source. Fluorescent bulbs reflect light off the ceiling for subtle general illumination; chrome spotlights focus beams on the countertops to complement the effect.

This convenient built-in dining booth also furnishes attractive storage space for cookbooks.

ual style of eating our culture has adopted. After all, the formal dining room with sparkling chandelier is no place to snack on last night's leftover pizza, but a banquette breakfast nook is perfectly suited to such quick snacks and informal meals. Of course, a kitchen eating area has step-saving advantages in addition to a friendly, informal ambience.

If the kitchen already has an eating area, you may need to reconsider its design and placement along with the other elements of your remodel, as the possibilities for dining are abundant in the medium-sized kitchen.

Islands and peninsulas can usually do double duty as informal snack counters when equipped with stools of appropriate height; for sit-down table service, design part of the island counter surface at table height. If there is only a very small space for a separate table, creating a banquette may work well because there is no need for clearance space for chairs (being pulled up and pushed back from the table).

Can you convert an adjacent space such as the laundry room or service porch into a breakfast area? Making the best use of your home's space is a matter of enjoyment, as well as practicality and function. Granted, you need laundry facilities, but you can probably have a perfectly functional laundry area without

Light wood floors and wall and molding treatment unify this eating area—a converted laundry room—with the period style of the kitchen.

The table-height snack counter on this island allows for the use of standard chairs—which are often more comfortable than stools—and provides a work surface for junior chefs who cannot easily reach the standard-height counters.

Adjustable shelves for cookbooks and collectibles surround this spruce little desk center.

This counter-level desk also provides crucial landing space for items from the refrigerator.

placing laundry priority above dining convenience. Perhaps you can convert the laundry room to a breakfast area and still have a laundry center behind shuttered or closed doors. If you do convert a neighboring room into an eating area, keep it and the kitchen area unified in their design/decorating treatment.

Any corner offers an opportunity for a desk area/ planning center. An efficient planning center has file cabinets, telephone, and bookshelves for your editions of Larousse *Gastronomique* and Julia Child, perhaps even a home computer. Carrot peelings and computer printout do not mix well, however, so set up the desk area away from the kitchen work triangle.

As soon as you enlarge the kitchen/eating space, you change the scale and layout of the entire dualpurpose room. This may introduce the problems addressed in the next chapter about the large kitchen.

CHAPTER 5

The Large Kitchen

A generous addition to a modest existing kitchen produced this open-plan kitchen, which incorporates the heavier textures of brickwork and beams. A multi-purpose island houses a commercial cooktop, drop-in range, and auxiliary sink, as well as seating.

A large kitchen often is born when a small- or medium-sized kitchen invades and occupies neighboring rooms and outdoor space. The result can be a food fancier's delight. Plenty of room for the barbecue chef and the pastry chef to parade their talents without skirmishing with one another. Commercial appliances and storage larders sufficient to satisfy the appetites of a battalion. A place where play or homework activities can occur in the watchful but unimpeded presence of the chief cook. The large kitchen can even accommodate a team of caterers on hand to prepare a black-tie dinner for 200 or a garden buffet for the neighbors. Yet bigger is not necessarily better. Without careful planning (and usually the help of a professional kitchen designer), this dream can turn into a nightmare of wearisome extra steps from one work center to another. The challenge of creating a large kitchen is to keep it unified, both functionally and visually.

Creating Visual Harmony

• *What basic principles should guide the choice of decorative elements for a large kitchen?*

A large kitchen can be a delightful playground for the imagination, showcasing a mood of rural charm, contemporary sophistication, drama, excitement, cool reserve, or whatever taste dictates. Its size requires an interplay of color, pattern, and texture for visual appeal and to avoid the sterile look of vast, undifferentiated surfaces. The color spectrum from light to dark is at your disposal, although a dark palette requires quite a bit of natural light to carry the look. A large, bold, and colorful pattern can show to good effect in a large kitchen while dramatically accentuating the size of the room. On the other hand, you are not restricted to large patterns. A small pattern will act as a background and introduce color into the room, although the pattern itself will tend to get lost.

These guidelines on color and patterns apply not only to wall covering, but to floor and ceiling treatment as well. A large kitchen can readily sustain a bold pattern on the floor—say, a nice big checkerboard of vinyl tiles or hefty 12 by 12-inch ceramic tiles. To balance

the scale of the room overhead, you can establish a handsome visual cadence of large beams with exposed hardware, ridged ends, clipped corners, molding, or other details; they can be positioned parallel only or intersecting. And, in a large kitchen, you can further treat the ceiling surface between the beams with textured plaster for a provincial or Moorish look, with veneer brick, or with wallpaper.

In general, a large kitchen can carry the heavy textures of brick, stone, and rough-hewn wood more effectively than can the medium-sized or small kitchen. But striking effects can also be created with subtler textures such as lace, cotton, lightly textured plaster, and smooth woods and tiles. In selecting materials from the latter group, be sure to use a variety in order to sustain visual interest.

Because one of the primary reasons for having a large kitchen is to incorporate other functions, large kitchens often do multiple duty as family, game room, office, greenhouse, electronic entertainment center, etc. As centers of such varied activities, they require appropriate furnishings—sofas, loveseats, club chairs, hutches, and area rugs to define the separate spaces. In choosing these furnishings, be sure to keep their scale, color, pattern, and texture consistent with the decor of the rest of your home.

Enhancing Architectural Assets

• *What can be done to bring out the architectural beauty of a large kitchen?*

A large kitchen calls for a creative hand in treating the physical space itself, in order to attain balance and proportion appropriate to the size of the room. If a large kitchen is planned through the merger of neighboring spaces, for example, the windows will probably need to be enlarged to fit the new scale. As in kitchens of all sizes, a lovely addition might be a bay window to give the dining area a serene view of flowering shrubs, a greenhouse window to house kitchen herbs and foliage, or a skylight—scaled to the size of the room—to open up the vertical dimension.

Introducing varying heights on both the floor and ceiling can contribute appealing lines to the sculptural quality of the room. Raised or sunken floors become an effective way of distinguishing the cooking area from other areas of the kitchen or routing traffic to bypass the primary work areas. A recessed ceiling adds a note

Heavy structural beams contrast smartly with lean contemporary decor. A butcher block counter on the island is accented by the polished metal of the pot rack/lighting fixture.

*Subtle combinations of wood, plaster, tile, and small-print
cotton curtains create a unified, eye-catching decor.*

This compact computer center is tucked snugly out of the way of traffic and food preparation areas.

Tailored to the owner's specific requirements, this cabinet features a desk, pull-out typewriter shelf, and a television caddy that pulls out and swivels so that the set can be viewed from the breakfast area and the island dining bar.

Tradition Updated

A dark, cramped space burdened by a hodgepodge effect of various window heights was the predecessor of this spacious traditional kitchen. With the removal of several nonbearing interior walls, four small neighboring rooms merged graciously into one open and airy space large enough for a multipurpose dining area. Painted wood cabinetry, colored glass and brass lighting fixtures, and detailing were chosen to reflect the venerable architectural character of the home and combine with modern amenities and the bold use of color to create an atmosphere at once classic and contemporary.

The new, efficient floor plan centers around a cooking peninsula. Its rounded counter extends the work space and lends a sculptural quality to this practical food preparation surface where the cook or a companion can sit comfortably on a stool.

The cooking peninsula features a down-draft cooktop, affording an unhindered view of the dining area beyond. Picture molding creates an even perimeter, unifying the irregular heights of windows and cabinets.

Small appliances hide behind a tambour door beneath the microwave oven, both of which are located conveniently close to the peninsula counter surface. To the rear, ovens and refrigerator frame a pull-out pantry. Extending behind the dining area, a 30-inch-high Corian counter doubles as a serving buffet and planning center.

A natural oak floor finished in a medium tone moderates the crisp contrast of imported dark green tiles on the peninsula counter, sprucely trimmed with white Corian.

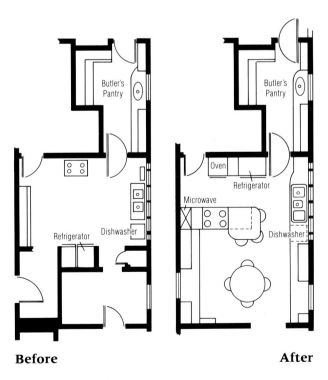

Updating the original butler's pantry included removing a useless coat of paint that covered the glass on the cabinet doors. The style of these cabinets provided the model for cabinetry throughout the kitchen.

Before

After

of formal grace. For a provocative interplay on the vertical plane, use a standard-height ceiling over the cooking area, which opens up in stunning angles to the roof over the dining or family gathering area.

A variation on this idea is to build a loft overlooking the kitchen. A loft can be used in many ways—as a library, a fine arts studio, a guest sleeping area, office, gallery, or television viewing area.

If it suits the overall style, a fireplace can be especially effective in providing the physical and emotional warmth the large space may call for. The fireplace can be incorporated into the cooking area itself and be used for indoor barbecuing or as a comforting backdrop for the dining table.

An on-site, masonry-built fireplace, which is lovely and authentic, is an expensive major structural installation. A masonry-built fireplace requires special footings to support the weight of the brick or stone chimney construction. Prefabricated fireplaces are available that can be finished with tile, stone, marble, textured plaster,

wood paneling, or mirrors. If cost or structural factors prohibit a "real" fireplace, consider the models that do not actually burn wood; the illusion of a crackling fire is produced by a flaming gas jet. In making your decision, remember that both wood-burning fireplaces, masonry-built and prefabricated, mean that you will be faced with the chores of keeping wood on hand, removing ashes, and occasionally cleaning the flue.

Arches have long been popular, especially over cooktops. A well-positioned arch of plaster, brick, or tile can create a handsome frame for hefty commercial ranges, cooktops, griddles, or barbecue grills while skillfully concealing the ventilation ducts for such appliances. Like a masonry-built fireplace, a masonry-built arch or one that supports any part of the structure of the house requires special footings sunk into the ground to carry the weight. If the arch serves only decorative, rather than structural, functions you can simply construct a wood frame, finished with brick, tile, or stone, without doing major structural work.

*The coupling of the original kitchen with an adjacent din-
ing room produced this airy, country-flavored kitchen—a
visually unified continuous space enhanced by the massive
plaster and wood fireplace in the dining area (opposite).
Above, graceful arched wine storage over antique pantry
doors repeats the curve of recessed shelves.*

Urban Innovations

An assortment of problems proved the inspiration for this uncommon contemporary kitchen. The spacious plan began as several small rooms, plagued with bad ventilation, awkward lighting, and a cumbersome structural column rising amid the walls. Removing the walls left the cooking area and original plumbing intact, while extensive remodeling incorporated numerous amenities, including six cabinets of pantry storage, a built-in eating area, and work centers arranged to foster the smooth flow of work and access to storage.

Making the most out of a liability, the structural column remains as a central design element, hand-somely turned out in wood finish to blend with the decor. Soffits now house efficient recessed lighting canisters as well as ventilation and air conditioning ductwork. An unusual loft living and play area was designed to provide access to a new spiral staircase leading to a room upstairs.

Recessed above the breakfast table, the loft overlooks the main work area—an L-shaped configuration modified by a cooking island. Rich wood finishes and metal accents embellish the subtle shading of plastic laminate cabinetry and contrasting laminate countertops. Front panels added to the existing refrigerator match the custom-made cabinets. A bank of dimmer switches to the left provides precision control of lighting effects.

The curved edge of the sink counter repeats the contours of the support column and the tapered cooking island. These rounded edges guide traffic effortlessly through the main thoroughfare and eating area. Soffits hide ductwork while creating visual interest overhead.

Soffit lighting above overhead cabinets highlights cabinet interiors when the doors are open, while undercabinet lighting illuminates countertop work areas. Window surveys an interior courtyard, one of many vistas deliberately created through the architectural nature of the design.

Behind the built-in eating area, a spiral staircase leads to the loft area and upper floor beyond. The loft provides a close but out of the way play space for children, when a parent is working in the kitchen. Laundry appliances are located under the loft.

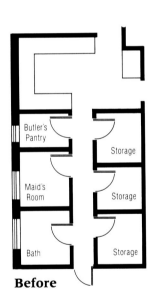

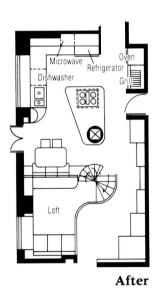

Before

After

In an unusual layout, the island accommodates the cooktop and ample landing space on the wide end, while tapering toward the structural column. Stepped-back cabinets underneath follow the contour. Unlike standard strip flooring, the herringbone pattern of the hardwood floor does not guide the eye in any one direction, which is an important consideration in a design as strongly geometric as this one.

Textures and architectural elements carry out a country theme in this robust kitchen. Both structural and surface-mounted beams add their rustic appeal to the textured straw and plaster ceiling. Imported, hand-painted tiles with a delicate floral pattern decorate the walls.

Possibilities for Minor Refurbishing

• *What improvements can be made in a large kitchen with limited remodeling and a limited budget?*

The frank truth is that a large kitchen usually dictates a thoroughgoing revamping, especially if it was originally formed by combining smaller rooms. The work required to adjust the scale and unify the spaces almost inevitably amounts to a major remodel, even when you are just adding a new window. If you think you will just tinker a bit with the wall coverings, you can easily wind up in a project of much larger scope simply because there are so many elements to coordinate. Changing any one element tends to have a domino effect on all the others. Cheerful new wall coverings may leave the floor looking dreary by contrast. If you then decide to replace the floor, the time may seem ripe for rethinking the layout—which, of course, brings into question the appropriateness of your present appliances. And so on down the garden path until the entire kitchen is redone anyway, but probably not as well as if you had planned a major remodeling at the outset.

With that caveat aside, however, if your large kitchen is basically well designed but falls short on visual appeal, a minor remodeling can yield a rich harvest of effects. Take a favorite theme—say, a French country motif—and execute it to its fullest. French doors make a handsome statement that can be echoed to good effect in glass-paned cabinet faces. Other additions might include hand-painted imported tiles on the backsplash, lace window curtains, dark beams against a textured-plaster ceiling, provençal-patterned paper on the walls, and copper cookware.

Customize kitchen cabinetry by planning organized compartments to avoid clutter. Install pull-out shelves on glides, lazy Susan shelves in corner cabinets.

*This kitchen was carefully scaled to
the large new greenhouse window.*

*Mullioned cabinet doors echo the
French doors and windows that
frame a view of the patio. The glass
on the cabinet doors enhances the
spacious, open feeling while providing
a counterbalance to the brick flooring.*

Matching arches house a full complement of commercial equipment. Each alcove has its own heavy-duty exhaust system for better ventilation. The brick column separating the alcoves conceals a support post. Tile interiors provide an insulating, easy-to-clean surface.

Convert an unused closet for pantry storage with narrow door shelves for easy access to often-used items. Create "garages" for small appliances where they are handy, protected, and out of the way. Add extra cabinets wherever unused space beckons. Install undercabinet lighting to illuminate countertops, cooktop, sink, and other work surfaces. Incorporate butcher block or hardwood chopping surfaces and marble surfaces for pastry dough. And, most important, organize your equipment, utensils, and supplies into their respective work centers, duplicating them if necessary, so that you do not waste energy walking over to the cooking area for spices or utensils needed in the baking area. Nutmeg and egg beater in the baking center; oregano, slotted spoons, spatulas, and garlic press at the cooktop. A wire whisk for each area. In a large kitchen where work centers tend to be spread out, such careful organization is crucial to overall effectiveness.

Cookbooks and dishes find housing in a cabinet tucked into an odd and otherwise unusable corner.

Going for Broke

• *When facing a major remodeling of a large kitchen, how can the seemingly limitless possibilities be focused into a rational plan and procedure?*

A large kitchen places few physical limits on what you can do with it. Therefore, the challenge of decision making rests primarily on you and your family. What do you need and what do you want? The answers to both these questions will require thought and research. A clipping file is useful at this point. Begin clipping pictures of appealing kitchen features and styles to serve as a guide in working out your own concept and for communicating it to your designer or kitchen planner.

This narrow space between two doors provides shallow storage for condiments and spices.

*Plumbing, electrical, and ventilation elements are hidden
in this handsome cylindrical column, which provides a
striking architectural focus accented by a metal pot rack.*

Separate refrigerator and freezer service a large family of hearty eaters. Traffic patterns and the position of doorways suggested the unusual shape of this open design.

Bear in mind that the design may be influenced by unalterable structural elements.

The next step is to analyze carefully the precise needs your kitchen must fulfill. Do you rely heavily on canned and dry foods for meal preparation? If so, generous pantry storage will be an important requisite. If you like to prepare a week's worth of meals in advance on the weekend, you will probably want a separate, full-sized freezer in your kitchen. If your taste runs to fresh vegetables and fruits, concentrate on vented vegetable bins and a separate salad preparation area.

Is there a characteristic trend in your cooking? Do your meals come primarily off the stove or out of the oven? Depending on the answer, you may wish to incorporate an extra cooktop, separate ovens, a griddle, a barbecue, a rotisserie, a wok, or any of the choices available to today's kitchen remodeler. If there are other cooks in your family, what are their special equipment needs? If your family includes two primary cooks who enjoy exercising their culinary talents in tandem, consider planning two distinct work triangles overlapping at the refrigerator.

What about entertaining? Do you like to include your guests in the meal preparation so that you can chat while one person deveins the shrimp, another operates the salad spinner, and a third decants the wine? If so, you had better plan an island and/or peninsula where the ménage à chefs can perform their duties. If you feel proprietary about the preparations, but do not like to be excluded from the social exchange, be sure to plan an informal social gathering area where your

In Harmony with Nature

A homeowner's penchant for entertaining sparked the transformation of a small, inefficient, poorly lit kitchen into this exemplary model of contemporary style, and in the process the room's shortcomings were adroitly converted into strengths. Where the original kitchen was marred by an intrusive corner chimney flue and inaccessible corner storage, the remodeled space (which incorporated an existing concrete pad from the porch to add approximately 100 square feet) matches the flue with full support columns in two of the other three corners, skirting the issue of corner storage altogether. A well-proportioned U-shaped work area around a central island now occupies the expanded space, while the opposite end of the room encompasses a spacious eating area, where guests can gather for hors d'oeuvres until the meal is ready.

The decorative elements of the kitchen, like the functional, have been executed with equal parts of innovation and care. Pastel lacquered cabinets match perfectly the molded laminate counters and knobs; all switches are on dimmer controls that respond to the touch of a fingertip; plug molding was used in place of conventional outlets, concealed under the overhead cabinets; windows are used in unique applications, bringing the outdoors inside.

An unusual windowed backsplash admits natural light above the sink while a floor-to-ceiling window reveals a wooded landscape facing the countertop desk area. At night these windows create a dramatic backdrop that contrasts with the pastel cabinets and counters abutting the structural column in the corner.

An interruption in the bank of base cabinets forms the desk area, underscoring the sense of openness created by the window.

Chimney flue is secreted in a closet (in foreground) and sheathed with narrow shelving for glassware storage. Bifold doors close off a pass-through between the bar area and the dining room beyond.

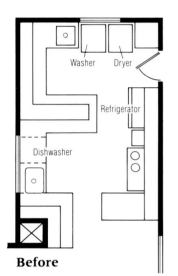

Before

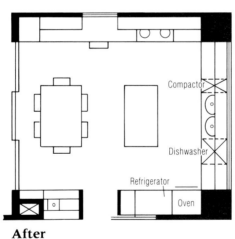

After

Painstaking attention to detail is revealed in this specially adapted drawer front, which shields a junction box supplying electricity to the desk area.

Plug molding is artfully concealed between the cabinet bottoms and top of window, handy for powering small appliances without obstructing the lines of the design.

Designed to serve a party of 200, this large, unobstructed
kitchen promotes socializing while food preparation takes
place. The large central island equipped with a vegetable
preparation sink and a marble insert can accommodate
several volunteers.

This cozy banquette with recessed television invites informal gatherings of family and friends. The television is positioned for viewing from the cooking as well as from the eating area. The angled corner of the table creates a smooth passageway.

guests can have drinks and hors d'oeuvres while keeping you company. Another alternative is a closed-plan kitchen where caterers can work in complete privacy and out of view of the social gathering.

A large kitchen usually has a more intricate layout than its smaller counterparts because it has a greater number of elements—multiple sinks, cooktops, and work centers. The primary food preparation center establishes the basic work flow from storage to mixing, cooking, and serving as outlined in chapter one. In a large kitchen, an island housing a cooktop, sink, or both may be a necessary convenience for pulling the work centers together. A large kitchen also offers the opportunity for auxiliary work stations for baking, barbecuing, or whatever pleases your fancy. As a general rule, each center should be as completely equipped as possible for its particular duties. You will probably need to acquire additional, even duplicate, cookware to equip the new work stations properly. Anyone accustomed to working in a smaller kitchen will be surprised at the

adjustment needed to cook comfortably in a large one. At first, you may wonder, with all of these cooktops and sinks, where do I prepare my tea? Fortunately, this sort of thorny dilemma is short lived, and whatever awkwardness may be present at first diminishes rapidly as you use your new large kitchen.

Because activities beyond cooking and eating come into the large kitchen's welcoming ambience, it is important to define separate areas to prevent collisions. If you wish to include an informal family gathering area, surrounding a hearth or big-screen television with hi-fi and video game components, a different floor or ceiling height will help differentiate the area. An island or other type of divider also works well. An office area must be planned thoroughly, with desk, typewriter, computer, and files well out of the main thoroughfare and cooking area so that you do not find your floppy discs and other supplies overflowing to food preparation surfaces. Another popular option for friends of the botanical kingdom is a section of the kitchen devoted to

This well-devised layout features an expansive island with seated preparation area, cooktop, and sink.

greenhouse duty. Foliage can be an attraction and a joy in a kitchen, but adding plants may require alterations to your windows or perhaps the addition of a solarium.

If you are including space for young children, plan storage for their games and toys and use a resilient floor covering that prevents skinned knees and other hard-floor injuries while also shrugging off occasional spills from the paint pot. An adult game center also requires special storage for housing a poker table or chess board plus sundry video games, the backgammon set, Parchesi board, and so on. In all of these cases, the kitchen functions as a cooking enclave within a larger multi-purpose area. Dining, playing, and other social activities take place around the perimeter, out of the way of cooking tasks. Yet, the open plan allows the kitchen workers to be included in family fun going on nearby. Multi-purpose use of a kitchen is as limitless as people's preferences and needs. What is crucial at this stage is for you to recognize your ideals and account for them in the planning.

Dutiful Auxiliaries

• *What additions can be made to the basic work triangle in a large kitchen?*

The most common types of secondary work centers are those set aside for cleanup, mixing and baking, salad preparation, and barbecuing. On a grander scale, a large kitchen can sometimes house a whole secondary kitchen for the two-chef family or a separate space for caterers.

The most all-around practical adjunct is a station for handling cleanup chores. Ideally, such an area is equipped with dishwasher, single sink, garbage disposer, and trash compactor, plus storage for cleaning products—sponges, scrub brushes, detergents, etc.—and storage cabinets for dishes, glassware, flatware, serving pieces, and table linens. Plan dishwasher placement and dish storage so that you can reach overhead cabinet shelves easily even when the dishwasher door is down for unloading dishes. For this reason, avoid positioning

The union of three rooms transformed a tiny corridor kitchen into this spacious open configuration, designed to include a play area for children where adult eyes can keep watch while the meal is on the stove.

the dishwasher in a corner. Overhead cabinets are not the only place for dish storage. Pull-out drawers are remarkably convenient for heavy dinnerware because it is much easier to lift heavy china out of drawers than to bring it down from shelves above.

The cleanup station is best located near the dining area to facilitate table setting and clearing. If your cleanup station consists of an island or divider between the cooking and dining areas, perhaps dinnerware can be stored in cabinets accessible from both sides. On the cleanup side china and glassware can be easily unloaded from the dishwasher and put away; on the dining side they can be removed from the cabinet and set on the table.

A separate bake center is a blessing for bakers and pastry chefs, particularly those of the younger gener-

ation. Whipping up a batch of Tollhouse cookies is a favorite form of after-school recreation in many families. A separate mix and bake center can help keep chocolate chips and walnut pieces out of your sauce Béarnaise or steak tartare.

A bake center is best located right next to ovens and, if possible, near the refrigerator as well, for access to milk, butter, and eggs. Depending on the other needs of your layout, you might put the bake center on the counter space between the two appliances. In any case, plan to include a single-compartment sink for adding water to dough and for washing off measuring spoons and cups. You will also need storage for flours, sugars, nuts, and spices needed for baking. Plan storage for mixing bowls and utensils, plus the mixer, blender, and food processor. Finally, the countertops should include wood surfaces for cutting and for rolling out pie doughs and a marble, granite, or Corian surface for preparing flake doughs. These can be installed as countertop inserts, pullout boards, or slabs cut to fit into the tops of drawers. If you like to work with butter doughs, you might find it helpful to have a marble slab cut to fit on a shelf in your refrigerator. The slab can be moved in

Roll-out shelves are an uncommon yet highly efficient method of dish storage that reduces the stretching and bending required to get at the dinnerware.

Hand-painted tiles project a country theme in this auxiliary cooking and cleanup niche.

Dish and glassware storage—attractively displayed behind framed glass doors—is conveniently located next to the cleanup center.

Located next to the secondary sink, this corner bake center includes ovens, housing for small appliances, and a recess for a microwave, plus storage for baking utensils, equipment, spices, and dry ingredients.

and out of the refrigerator as needed without disturbing the dough.

Another enjoyable addition to the large kitchen is a barbecue center for turning out authentic hot links, down-home chicken, and ribs to compete with Kansas City's finest. For greatest convenience, a barbecue center also should be close to the refrigerator and equipped with a single sink and disposer, storage for barbecue tools, and plenty of countertop on both sides of the cooking unit. Many indoor barbecuers like to enclose their grill in a brick arch for an outdoor cooking grotto effect. Such an enclosure often lacks space for handy chopping surfaces, however, requiring the chef to traipse back and forth from the grill to the countertop. Butcher block provides a good surface for chopping, but remember that any wood, no matter how hard, is still porous and will absorb meat and vegetable juices. If you install butcher block countertops, they will not remain pristine forever; in the course of normal use, butcher block shows stains and wear. An alternative is to use portable butcher blocks. One type fits over the sink and comes equipped with a hole for pushing discards into the disposer. Another is a chopping block table that rolls out of the way when not in use. For average-height people, a butcher block pull-out board installed at drawer level (instead of standard counter height) may provide better leverage for cutting. Or, for the king-sized barbecue chef, you can get a butcher block on rubber feet. Placed on top of the counter, this option offers better cutting leverage. Some cooktops have butcher blocks that fit over them when they're not in use.

A household with two serious cooks calls for dual kitchens. Organize each mini-kitchen around the particular needs of the individual cook. Once the functional elements are in place, tie the spaces together visually through the finish materials, colors, textures, and scale. The two spaces should seem like a unified whole, not the front line in the Battle of the Bulge.

Maxi-Storage for Food Staples

• *How can a large kitchen's ample room for food storage best be utilized?*

Walk-in storage rooms are throwbacks to the past that have recently come back into vogue, and they are ideal for large kitchens. Plan to convert a section of your kitchen into a walk-in pantry, cooler, or larder.

Each provides a large volume of storage for food supplies on hand. A cooler draws air in from the basement or crawl space through a vent in the floor and out through another vent in the ceiling, while a pantry does not. The cooler's temperature remains cooler than that of the rest of the house, and, equipped with slatted or wire shelving for optimal circulation, a cooler is a prime place to keep fresh fruits and vegetables. A larder is insulated and thermostatically controlled. You can effectively enclose your pantry, cooler, or larder with glass doors and walls, which will give the kitchen a feeling of spaciousness. The colorful labels on packages and cans also contribute a lively and charming note to certain kitchen styles.

Of course, walk-in storage rooms require interior light—a consideration that's equally important if you simply want to convert a large closet for pantry storage. When adapting a closet, be sure that interior shelves are no more than 12 to 15 inches deep, to allow easy access. If the closet is deep enough, you can install 5-inch shelves on the inside of the door to hold a single row of useful items. Don't hesitate to combine various storage features such as pull-out, swing-out, and adjustable shelves.

Another popular storage idea is the home wine cellar, which is a welcome replacement for the wine rack over the refrigerator (a poor place to keep wine) or in some corner of the kitchen. Such racks may be pleasing to look at, but they are hardly suitable for bringing out the best in your vintage St. Emilion, which requires a cool, strictly controlled temperature. For a proper wine cellar, you might convert yet another one of those miscellaneous closets. Insulate the walls, fit it with racks for storing bottles on their sides, and equip it with a thermostat-controlled refrigeration device. If you have run out of extra closets by now, you can purchase a ready-made wine cabinet equipped with racks and refrigeration. These units are usually 24 inches wide and 3 to 6 feet high.

Oversized Equipment

• *What considerations apply to the choice of commercial appliances for home use?*

You have the space, and you and your large family like to entertain large numbers of guests. Go commercial. Such appliances can handle a high volume of sophisticated use. Instead of the standard four-burners,

This oak pantry with chicken wire framed in the doors displays a spirited medley of product containers that lend a charming country ambience to the kitchen.

Door shelves and hinged storage panels make the most of available space in this generous full-height pantry.

A deft combination of stationary, pull-out, and swing-out shelves maximizes the storage volume in this cabinet.

ranges and cooktops offer up to twelve burners, plus a separate griddle for blueberry hotcakes and a grill for burgers and steaks. A commercial refrigerator unit can give you many times the volume of storage that a standard residential models can. But remember that commercial appliances have different requirements than residential models, both mechanically and physically. For example, a commercial range is usually too large to be moved through standard-size doors. It also gives off much more heat both during operation and when not in use and puts an additional load on the air conditioning system. It requires you to cover the installation cavity with fireproof, heat-resistant material, such as ceramic tile, brick, or stone, and the surrounding cabinets should be lined with heat-retardant building material as well. When shopping for a commercial range, look for one with a pilotless ignition feature that cuts down on the fuel consumed and heat generated. Installation of commercial equipment requires the participation of an experienced professional to ensure that the plumbing, ventilation, and structural elements are properly and safely adapted to handle the new load.

Stainless steel counters flanking the commercial range enhance the industrial look established by the range and provide an ideal landing surface for cookware coming hot from the oven.

CHAPTER 6

Plan into Action

This stylish kitchen started out as a bedroom, a major remodeling effort that required meticulous planning and coordination of work flow.

Putting your plans on paper is the first step on the route from fantasy to fruition. A floor plan drawn to scale will enable you to play with your layout two-dimensionally, moving the cabinets, refrigerator, and other elements around on the page until you discover the optimum arrangement. A color board showing samples of finish materials gives you a reading on the harmony of colors, textures, and patterns, allowing you to weed out any hideous mismatches before a fateful step is taken. Practical, nitty-gritty details of translating ideas into actuality follow.

Drafting a Functional Floor Plan

• *What, exactly, is the purpose of making a floor plan, and how does one proceed?*

If you are redesigning your kitchen yourself, you must make a floor plan to ensure that the brilliant products of thought and imagination are actually workable in the hard realm of physical reality. Through your floor plan you may find out, for example, that what seemed like an ingenious arrangement of work centers does not allow you to open the refrigerator door at an angle greater than 90 degrees. Or that there is no passage space when oven and dishwasher doors are open at the same time. The floor plan is the essential link between fantasy and fact. It gives you a chance to try out your ideas before making a commitment you'll have to live with later or change at added expense.

If you are working with a designer, of course, he or she will be developing a floor plan and blueprints for the contractor. Drafting your own floor plan can help to clarify and communicate your ideas to the designer, but it is certainly not essential that you do so.

To make a floor plan, you will need ¼-inch graph paper, tracing paper, soft-lead pencil, ruler, clipboard, a steel tape measure, and templates of cabinets and

appliances in various sizes, which can be purchased at an art supply store. Begin by measuring the perimeter of the room, noting the exact locations and dimensions of windows and doors and any plumbing, electrical, or other features that must remain. Using a scale of ½ inch = 1 foot, transfer the measurements and angles onto graph paper so that you have an accurate bird's-eye-view drawing of the room with all permanent features properly represented.

Now, place a sheet of tracing paper over the outline of the room, and, using the templates, trace cabinets and appliances according to your concept, making sure to account for necessary storage and counter surface in each work center. Remember that moving the sink will add significantly to the cost of the project. Unless you have compelling reasons for changing its location and a large remodeling budget, it is best to begin with the sink as the one fixed element and build your new work triangle around it.

If the first draft of your plan looks too crowded, you have the choice of expanding the space into adjoining rooms and niches or cutting down on the internal features. Perhaps you must relinquish the six-burner commercial range with griddle and grill and use a standard four-burner residential unit, or try out the compact, consolidated units mentioned in chapter three. If room consolidation seems like the best solution, measure the dimensions of the potential addition and draw an aerial view of the proposed expanded space, using it as an outline for playing with the elements of your layout. If, on the other hand, the new layout leaves work centers too widely scattered (more than 22 feet apart), sketch in an island to pull them together.

Feel free to shift the positions of doors and windows to try improving traffic patterns or to enhance the natural light. But keep in mind how the changes would affect the exterior of your house. Such modifications might work well at the rear but not at all in front or at the side of the house. Consider angled counters, or some other unusual arrangement, using a fresh tissue overlay for each layout draft. The floor plan is a playground for the imagination where you have the freedom to try out daring ideas without taking any risks. Do not censor your ideas at this point; tracing paper is cheap. In the end, you will have a series of drafts from which to choose. If the final selection is not obvious from the functional merits of one particular draft, a consultation with a designer may be in order.

Reconciling the Aesthetics

• *What role does the color board play in planning?*

A color board is a mat board about 30 by 36 inches, which displays samples of every finish material and every decorative item you have chosen for your new kitchen. These include samples of paint finishes, wall covering, flooring, stain or cabinet finish, counter and backsplash materials, cabinet hardware, fabric, molding, window treatments, brick/stone/masonry as appropriate, photographs of light fixtures, and any special decorative features such as etched glass or tile mosaics. Free samples of colors, stains, textures, and patterns are usually available from suppliers.

The color board gives you an opportunity to study the final conglomerate of finishes to see how the elements blend with one another—in terms of subtleties of the palette, authenticity of the chosen period or style, and the overall mood. Is the cabinet stain too dark for the pale Sante Fe tones on the walls or does it provide

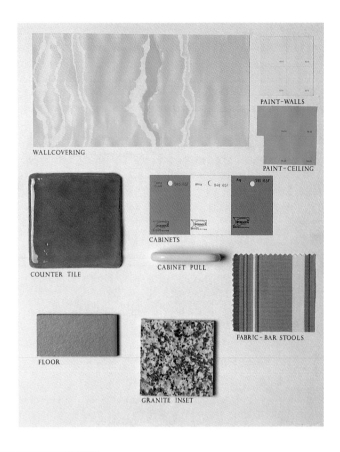

Color boards for two distinct styles of decor, country and contemporary, indicate how the decorative elements of each will go together.

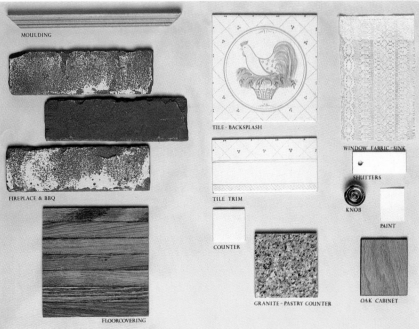

a welcome contrast? Does the cheerful printed fabric for the windows enhance the country feeling or is the pattern too contemporary? Examine each finish material as it relates to the total look; experiment by substituting other color chips or pattern samples if you are uncertain or dissatisfied. Just as your floor plans let you play with spatial ideas, this is your chance to fine tune the aesthetics before making final decisions.

The color board also indicates the location and use of each finish material in the new kitchen. Once you have finalized your choices, the color board serves to specify your exact wishes to your contractor and subcontractors: terra cotta hexagonal pavers covering 4 by 12 feet of floor; antique oak stain on the cabinets; 3-inch glazed ceramic tiles, eggshell, on all counter surfaces; and so on. In communicating with your contractor, the color board should be accompanied by specification sheets listing the material, finish, manufacturer, relevant dimensions, and model or identification number of the material. The specification sheets, available from suppliers, will ensure that you do not wind up with walnut herringbone parquet squares where you wanted the noble simplicity of tongue-and-groove planks. Be sure to get a specification sheet for each person who is to work with a particular material or to bid on the work. Specification sheets will be used for estimates and for installation. From the individual specification sheets, make up a master list for yourself, your contractor, and subcontractors, itemizing every new element of your kitchen and stating the manufacturer, the model number, the material, color or finish, the source, if known, and any other relevant information.

Professional Input

* *What is the client's role in relation to the designer and/or builder?*

As mentioned in chapter two, the amount of professional help you will need depends on the complexity of the job and your level of skill in matters of interior design and construction. By all means, do not fall into the trap of underestimating the needs of the job. Even a fresh coat of paint requires more than just a few brush strokes. Nicks and other blemishes must

first be meticulously patched and sanded in order to get an even finish. The do-it-yourself cost savings are paid for dearly with your time, which always turns out to be exponentially greater than you imagine at the outset.

A professional planner is something of a buffer against the harsher realities of remodeling. To plan and cost out the work accurately, the planner will need to know your budget for the job (remember to allow a margin for upcharges), your thoughts about the assets and liabilities of your present kitchen (review chapter two), your priorities of function and style (show your file of picture clippings), and other relevant information influencing the activities in your kitchen such as work habits, entertaining style, and your children's ages.

If a general contractor is doing the work without the aid of a designer or planner, you will need to supply your floor plan, color board, and specification sheets for all materials as the basis for figuring the bid. Solicit bids from three contractors, preferably those with solid professional references. Be sure to supply each contractor with identical information and specifications so that each bid covers the same plan and materials.

In comparing the three estimates, look for and ask about any hidden costs that have not been accounted for. Does the cost of the cabinetry include the finish work? Do the prices quoted for new appliances include installation? Will the new greenhouse window require an adjustment of your home security system? Does the new range pose any special venting problems not reflected in the bid? In choosing among contractors, also consider the timetable for completion proposed by each and their availability—can they start the job as soon as you are ready?

The general contractor orchestrates the work of the various subcontractors. This can be an extremely subtle and demanding business—making sure, for example, that if the tile subcontractor is scheduled to lay down the countertop tiles on Wednesday, the wood molding trim has been installed, stained, and sealed by Tuesday. Or that the electrician has provided a finished electrical outlet in time for the plumber to install the garbage disposer. Seemingly minor slip-ups on the schedule can result in surprisingly long delays. With a competent general contractor in charge, there should be no need for you to be present on the job site supervising the work; nevertheless you should keep in close touch with your contractor to follow the course of progress and to learn about the problems that inevitably arise.

Substantial savings on the overall cost are available

to those with the time and expertise to subcontract out the work themselves. This involves supplying plans and specifications, taking bids from subcontractors in the relevant trades, hiring tradesmen, scheduling, coordinating, and supervising the work. It is no exaggeration to say that acting as your own contractor can turn into a monstrous task filled with surprising twists and turns for the unsuspecting novice. The specifics involved in contracting a remodeling job go well beyond the scope of this book. Unless you are already skilled and experienced in this capacity, it is best to turn the responsibility over to a qualified professional.

Whatever level of responsibility you assume on the project, it is crucial for you to inspect the work periodically and discuss the progress—or lack of it—with your contractor or the appropriate tradesman. Such consultations communicate your concern about the orderly flow of work. Inspections allow you to catch mistakes before they multiply and cause costly delays. If a skylight turns out to be too small, for example, it should be corrected immediately rather than later, after other work on the ceiling has been completed. Inspect the job at the framing stage, when the electrical and plumbing lines have been roughed in but before they are sealed off behind wallboard or plaster. Go over the plans with your contractor and/or designer to make certain that all systems have been accounted for. Inspect again after the walls are finished to see that electrical outlets, switches, vents, and plumbing pipe stubs have not been sealed over and that they are properly connected.

tractor, he will be familiar with the local building code and will obtain the permits as part of his job. If you are not working with a contractor, call the local building inspector or city planning agency for the required information, including the length of time it takes to get the permits. In small communities, the process usually takes from two days to a week. In large metropolitan areas, especially where there are actively watchful homeowners' associations, the process can take up to two months. Electrical and plumbing subcontractors can obtain permits for their work. In this case, be sure to find out whether the cost of pulling the permits is included in their bids.

The inevitable result of applying for permits is a series of on-site visits from the local building inspector, whose duty is to make sure that the work complies with the building code. His visits will coincide with the completion of different stages of work. If you are undertaking major structural work such as building an addition, the inspector will stop by first to check and sign off the new foundation. At the next stage, he will inspect all of the rough work: framing, electrical, and plumbing. His last visit will be to inspect the finish work to see that the electrical and plumbing fixtures have been properly connected. If the permits and inspections seem like a burden at times, it may be comforting to remember that their purpose is to ensure the quality and safety of the work going into your home. You will soon forget the annoyance once it is over, and you will have a reasonable assurance that your house will not suddenly go up in flames because of an incompetent wiring job.

Your Local Building Code

• *What procedures are required in order to comply with building codes?*

Each community has its own code and procedures governing building construction. These codes do not apply to simple redecorating, but they do apply to electrical, plumbing, and construction work, and you must obtain the appropriate building permits before construction can begin. If you have hired a general con-

Preparing for the Onslaught

• *How do you cope with preparing meals while your kitchen is under construction?*

If your remodeling plan involves changing the cabinetry, appliances, or rearranging the layout, you will have to set up a temporary kitchen for the duration. No matter how tempting their variety, the offerings of local take-out restaurants will probably not see you through the ordeal. Establish your temporary kitchen in some part of the house where you have access to water, if possible, plus space for setting up vital equipment such as your refrigerator, a hotplate, coffee maker, slow cooker, and microwave oven. Good candidates are a separate dining room or sun porch with nearby powder room, or even a garage with a utility sink. If running water is not available in your temporary quarters, a water cooler with hot and cold spigots is a handy substitute, although it does not work well for cleanup.

Make a complete inventory of your kitchen equipment and utensils. Select the essential tools for your temporary kitchen—paring knife, chopping knife, carving knife, cutting surface, bottle opener, mixing and measuring utensils, pots and pans, large fork and spoon, table service (or paper plates and plastic "silverware"), hand towels, dish towels, potholders, napkins, spices and basic food staples, a broom, bucket and dishpan for doing the dishes, detergent, garbage can, and any other necessary cleaning products. Pack the rest in labeled boxes for storage until the remodeling is completed.

You will need a makeshift work surface such as the type of long, folding table available from rental companies. Make sure to get one with a hard, smooth, easy-to-clean surface. Using bricks or cinder blocks and boards, make a shelf on top and at the back of the table for spices and basic food staples. Place pots, pans, glasses, and dishes below the shelf. Larger items can be stored in boxes beneath the table. Set up your various small cooking appliances on the table itself. A slow cooker, toaster oven, and even microwave can really earn their keep during this period, allowing you to turn out surprisingly substantial hot meals without your customary cooktop and ovens. Finally, be sure to provide floor lamps and table lamps to keep your work area properly illuminated, preventing eye strain and mishaps.

No matter how skillfully and sensibly your temporary kitchen is arranged, there will be moments when its limitations take their toll on your nerves. At such times, remember that once remodeling is done, these trials will swiftly fade into distant memory as you delight in the joys of your new kitchen.

Close-ups and Options

There was a time in the not-too-distant past when every up-to-date kitchen had painted cabinets, laminated plastic or tile counters, linoleum floors, chrome hardware, and one overhead light fixture. Appliances generally ran to a gas or electric range, refrigerator-freezer, garbage disposer, and toaster. Artistic impulses most often found expression through paint and wallpaper.

Today's homeowner, by contrast, is presented with an exhilarating array of products and materials for creating a functional and stylish kitchen. But that wealth of options can be as bewildering as it is liberating.

The following pages highlight the properties of selected products, materials, and custom options you should consider while your new kitchen is still on the drawing board. The choices presented here, though wide, are just a beginning; your kitchen planner or designer can direct you toward others that may also be suitable for your kitchen—and your budget. But this browsing guide can help you start making the informed decisions that shape every well-planned and well-executed kitchen and, ultimately, ensure that your new kitchen fulfills all your needs.

Cabinets

A prime beneficiary of design technology, kitchen cabinetry today offers function and grace in styles that capture and express the character of your kitchen. Whether custom-made or modular, traditional wood or sleek laminate, choices include a style for every mood, a design for every purpose. Finished wood and laminated plastic are the easiest surfaces to care for, as they just wipe clean. High-gloss lacquer must be buffed, but painted wood cabinets are the most difficult to maintain—they show dirt and fingerprints, and the finish is not impervious to abrasives.

Custom Cabinets

Custom cabinets provide a personalized approach to cabinetry design. Built by a cabinetmaker to your specifications, custom work can give you just what you want in size, style, design, and finish. It allows for specialized treatment of odd angles, corners, or nooks and for matching a specific period treatment in your home. In ordering custom units, specify interior and exterior finishes, hardware, and any special design features.

Solid walnut custom cabinetry

Laminated plastic custom cabinetry

Painted custom cabinetry

Lacquer-finish custom cabinetry

Modular Units

Manufacturers of modular units offer many of the practical options that custom cabinetry provides in a wide—though not unlimited—variety of styles and finishes. Some modular lines even come in custom sizes. Available from dealers, modular units still offer budget-minded prices on basic cabinetry, although those lines featuring custom options now compete with and even outstrip the cost of custom-made units.

Stained wood modular cabinetry

European lacquer-finish modular cabinetry

Wood modular cabinetry

Cabinetry Storage Features

The interior features of today's kitchen cabinetry utilize every inch of storage potential. In the sampling that follows, add-on, modular, and custom accessories offer streamlined convenience and efficient organization of tools and utensils. The various modular cabinet lines offer different interior features. If you are planning to use modular cabinets, consult the manufacturers' catalogs for specific options.

Spice Storage

Shallow cabinet storage

Wall storage

Swing-out cabinet storage

Spice drawer

Wall storage

Spice storage on cabinet door

Pantry with adjustable pull-out shelves and automatic interior light

Pull-out pantry storage for a deep, narrow space

Full pantry storage featuring three doors, vegetable bins, narrow spice storage, and full pull-out shelves, with partitioned storage above.

Full pantry with pull-out shelves

Pull-out pantry functioning as spacer between appliances

Pantry with swing-out shelves

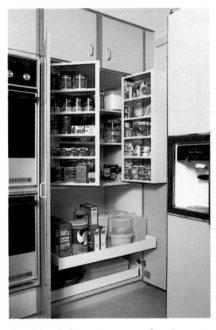

Combined deep storage and swing-out shelves

Cooler cabinet with slatted shelves

Pantry storage with antique doors

Pantry with chicken wire inserts in doors

Auxiliary Food Storage

Wire vegetable bins

Add-on vegetable bins positioned next to pull-out shelves

Pull-out food storage in base cabinet

Shallow food storage in unused corner (between doors)

Dish, Cookware, and Utensil Storage

Knife storage built into drawer

Drawers for tableware and pot storage, angled to fit into awkward space

Drawer partitioned and lined with Pacific Cloth for silver storage

Tall cabinet with adjustable and pull-out shelves and partitioned storage, for pots, linens, and trays

Deep drawer for pot storage

Knife storage built into butcher block counter

Full cabinet storage for pots and pans

Partitioned tray storage in base cabinet

Partitioned drawer for pot lids and small baking dishes

Partitioned storage for trays over oven

Pull-through dish storage for two-sided access

Dish storage in drawers

Utility Storage

Utility closet with overhead wine storage

Combined food and utility storage for saving space

Corner Cabinet Access

Pull-out and swing-out shelves

Open shelving in base cabinets

Half-round pull-out shelves

Lazy Susan (and wire vegetable bin)

Lazy Susan with piano-hinged door

Sink Cabinets

Racks mounted on cabinet doors

Recessed cabinet to accommodate knee space

Tilt-out compartment

Special Touches

Built-in planter with storage below

Open shelving with library ladder

Small Appliance Storage

Pop-up mixer shelf

Appliance garage with hinged door

Appliance garage with tambour door

Food-processing center on island

Appliance garage with bi-fold door

Carts

Manufactured mobile work center

Mobile cabinet

Serving cart

Islands and Peninsulas

These multipurpose work centers are designed to improve a kitchen's layout. Each can be used for a great variety of activities: as a cooking and serving center equipped with cooktop and dining bar; as a food preparation area with sink/disposer and butcher block counters; as a cleanup station with sink, dishwasher, and compactor, plus table service storage, or any combination of the above. When planning an island or peninsula, allow 42 inches of clearance on all exposed sides.

Peninsulas

Peninsula cleanup center separating kitchen from eating area

Angled peninsula incorporating kitchen work area

Peninsula with overhead storage

Peninsula with cooktop and storage above and below

Peninsula with cooktop and eating bar

Peninsula rounded to form additional work area

Islands

Island with eating area and marble top

Island 18 inches wide, with open storage below

Island with commercial cooktop and table extension

Asymmetrical island with cooktop and structural column, featuring stepped-back cabinetry to follow contours

Angled island to accommodate traffic

Island with sink and eating area, featuring channel in top for catching liquids

Angled island with sink

Large island with sink and food-processing center

Pass-Throughs

A pass-through is an above-the-counter passageway between the kitchen and an adjacent room or patio for convenient food service and cleanup between these areas. A pass-through usually screens off the kitchen with glass partitions, bi-fold doors, shutters, or other methods of concealment.

Pass-through to den; can be closed off with bi-fold doors

Pass-through to outside counter

Pass-through to butler's pantry

Pass-through to eating area

Pass-through to dining room, with movable glass partition

Eating Arrangements

A comfortable kitchen table with chairs is always desirable for step-saving serving and cleanup convenience. An eating nook's space requirements are at least 2 feet per person, as well as room for serving and for the passage of traffic. Where the clearance requirements of a table and chairs don't jibe with the available space, alternatives are a banquette, snack counter, or pull-out table.

Table and Chairs
A dining table arrangement needs at least 30 inches of clearance between the table and walls to allow diners to sit down and get up comfortably.

Table and chairs

Dining Bar
A worthy offspring of multipurpose design, the dining bar occupies space on a peninsula, island, or counter that easily doubles for food preparation, with stools or chairs efficiently tucked away. For a dining bar at standard table height (30 inches) use chairs for seating; at counter height (36 inches) use 24-inch stools; for a counter mounted at 42 inches (usually behind the cooktop or sink), use high stools, 30 to 36 inches.

Peninsula eating bar

Table extension as part of island

Eating area at island

Island eating area with enclosed knee space

Peninsula eating bar

Banquette

A banquette is a cozy, space-saving alternative for cramped quarters. With built-in seats on three sides, a banquette does not have to allow for chairs pushing back or for traffic to pass through at the rear.

Banquette with built-in book storage

Banquette

Pull-Out Tables

One of the deft developments of cabinet design is the extension table that pulls out from a base cabinet just like a pull-out board. A pull-out table offers intimate dining for two and can also double as counter space as the need arises. A pull-out board can also serve as an eating area.

Pull-out table

Full-extension counter

Counters

Tough, durable, easy-to-clean, yet pleasing to the eye, today's countertop materials strive to combine the virtues of workhorse and beauty queen. Because different materials have different properties, it's often wise to select two or three surfaces for specific functions: marble or granite in the baking center and butcher block in the food preparation area, for example.

Corian Corian, a petroleum-based synthetic marble, imitates the sleek, smooth surface of natural marble. Unlike granite or marble, Corian is easy to work with. It can be cut or carved with a saw to achieve unusual detailing and decorative effects. Ceramic tile edging supplies a striking trim. The versatility of Corian does not extend to its color range, which is limited to neutral tones.

Stainless Steel Used on counters and backsplashes, this material lends a certain drama to neo-modern kitchens, although it rates low marks in the area of practicality because its soft surface is easily blemished by scratches.

Granite The gleaming, speckled surface of granite offers all the benefits of marble plus easy maintenance and resistance to stains.

Laminated Plastic Available today in a satisfying range of colors, wood tones, and other patterns, laminate is a popular and practical choice for counter material. Invulnerable to most stains, somewhat resistant to heat and scratching, laminate comes with a postformed (molded) or square edge, which can be trimmed with other materials. Some laminated plastics cannot be formed or molded, however, and some are recommended for vertical surfaces only. Check with the dealer or manufacturer.

Marble Marble counters lend an air of nobility to a kitchen. Available in delicate colors, with a hard, cool texture, natural marble, like granite, is an excellent surface for pastry dough. Marble is, nonetheless, a porous material, easily marred by stains and difficult to clean.

Butcher Block The comforting warmth of hardwood butcher block counters enhances almost every decor. Butcher block provides a handy surface for chopping and slicing, although its surface is actually quite sensitive to moisture, stains, and scorching. A periodic rubdown with linseed oil offers limited protection.

Tile Available in a stunning variety of colors, patterns, glazes, and tinted grouts, tile offers a vast range of decorative effects along with the practical advantages of being resistant to heat and stains and easy to wipe clean. Tiles suitable for countertops should have a flat, square, and even surface so that delicate, footed glassware stands level. Any given tile may come with companion trim pieces. If not, wood, Corian, or cut tiles can provide a handsome frame. Be aware, however, that some tile should be used only in a vertical installation. Check with the dealer or manufacturer.

Floors

Today's abundant floor coverings strive to fulfill wide-ranging demands. Like other kitchen materials, floor covering should provide wearability, decorative appeal, and carefree maintenance. Moreover, and importantly, it must also be comfortable to walk on.

Carpet Available in solids, geometric and designer patterns, carpet gets the prize for resilient comfort underfoot. It also provides excellent insulation against cold and clamor. Synthetic fibers offer the greatest resistance to stains. For normal soil, vacuuming and occasional shampooing will preserve carpet's appearance, although spilled grease can cause quite a cleanup problem; hot grease or flame can even melt the fiber.

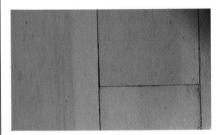

Soft Wood Planks of pine or fir enhance a country or early-American kitchen. However, the soft character of the wood makes it vulnerable to scratches, gouges, and other signs of wear. Because its looks do not hold up under heavy use, soft wood is not considered a cost-effective choice for kitchen flooring.

Hardwood A wood floor possesses a classic appeal that does not go out of style with shifting trends. Its hospitable warmth is available today in everything from traditional oak or maple to uncommon ash, padouk, or wenge, and in addition to standard strip configurations, a wealth of parquet patterns, as well as bleaches, stains, and finishes. A wood floor does require frequent attention with a vacuum, as its sleek surface—especially with a glossy finish—will mirror dust and lint. A matte finish is more concealing. Sealed with a moisture-curing urethane, wood floors are easy to maintain and do not require waxing. If heavy use erodes its beauty over the years, a refinishing treatment will restore a wood floor's looks to new.

Rubber Tiles The no-nonsense chic of rubber tiles finds a compatible home in high-tech or contemporary-style kitchens. Its studded, nonskid surface is easy on the feet, although rubber is sensitive to scuff marks and requires frequent treatment with soap and water, wax, or rubber polish. A normal kitchen mishap—dropping a hot frying pan, for example—can cause rubber to tear or even melt. On the other hand, china or glassware dropped on rubber flooring has a chance of surviving intact.

Brick and Stone An imperishable, practical, hard-surface flooring, brick can be laid in herringbone, parallel, and many other pleasing patterns. Unlike almost any other material, wear improves the character of brick. Like stone and ceramic tile, brick requires no special maintenance, although if unsealed, it will absorb grease and stains. Its hard surface also conducts noise and cold.

A stunning foundation, stone holds its beauty through the years, regardless of the amount of wear it gets. It is, nonetheless, an expensive and impractical choice for kitchen floors. Its cold, hard surface amplifies clatter and is hard on weary feet, and like brick, some stone is porous and can absorb stains. A dull-finish floor wax can counteract stain absorption to some degree, but it is by no means a complete solution. Furthermore, even a minor spill of grease or water turns stone slick and slippery.

Vinyl Tile and Sheet Goods Vinyl floor products today come in an almost boundless variety of styles, colors, textures, and patterns, including marble, wood, brick, ceramic tile, leather, slate, and rush fiber look-alikes. Of all floor covering materials, vinyl stands out in its combined practical virtues: long-lasting durability, easy upkeep (in many cases requiring no waxing), and resilient comfort for the feet, especially in styles that include cushioning.

Cushioned vinyl is difficult to install—the tiles tend to pop up—and should be handled by a professional. Sheet flooring, which comes on rolls, is also hard for do-it-yourselfers to install well. But because there are fewer joints than with tiles, it is somewhat easier to maintain. Vinyl tiles are easier to install than sheet flooring, and they are more flexible in terms of design, as they come in many shapes, sizes, colors, and designs, which can be mixed and matched.

Ceramic Floor Tile

Ceramic floor tile, long cherished for its natural beauty, is available in impressive variety. Selections include graphic grids, rich and subtle contemporary tones, folk art designs for the charming base of a country theme. Ceramic floor tiles include glazed tiles in many sizes and shapes; the heftier, unglazed pavers; and tough, skid-resistant quarry tiles in natural earth tones such as sand or terra cotta. Unglazed tiles should be treated with sealer to resist stains. Tile is an expensive choice but price-worthy in its long-lasting durability and easy damp-mop maintenance, although it offers no insulation against noise or cold.

High-gloss ceramic tiles

Mexican pavers

Mosaic tiles

Wall Treatments

Wall treatment is a crucial choice influencing the spatial dynamics of a room. In a small room, light colors, small patterns, and subtle textures exaggerate the sense of space, whereas dark colors, large patterns, and heavy textures could have a suffocating effect. A large room, naturally, lends itself to bolder wall treatments.

A vertical pattern gives a sense of added space overhead, while a horizontal pattern opens up the width. Continuing a pattern from the walls to the ceiling will usually lower the ceiling. Materials such as wood, mirrors, and laminates can also hide bumps or gouges in the wall surface. Like other kitchen finish materials, a wall treatment has to stand up to heat, grease, and scrubbing with its looks intact.

Wallpaper This tried-and-true wall covering comes in a wide variety of colors and designs, in some cases pre-pasted with adhesive for convenience. A coat of varnish will seal the paper against most of the effects of kitchen wear. Vinyl wall covering comes in the form of paper impregnated with vinyl or polyvinylchloride on a cloth backing. Vinyl products rate especially high on durability since they can be wiped or scrubbed clean.

Ceramic Tile Imported or domestic, hand-painted or stock, ceramic tile offers an exciting range of contemporary, traditional, or country effects. Tile is durable and easy to clean, though sometimes costly.

Fabric A fabric wall covering can provide appealing textures and effects, but unless it is sealed with vinyl to repel grease and moisture, fabric is not a practical choice for the kitchen.

Paint Perhaps the humblest—and certainly the least expensive—of wall treatments, paint can nonetheless create a look of sophistication and elegance and offers a virtually unlimited choice of colors. By using a variety of applicators, you can vary the effects of paint, stippling, stenciling, and blotting it on the wall. Because it is easiest to keep clean, glossy or semi-gloss paint is better suited to kitchen walls than a flat finish.

Brick or Stone These rough, porous, and often expensive materials lend color and a rustic texture to kitchen walls. They can be hard to clean, although they are durable.

Ceiling Treatments

While the functional value of a ceiling is usually limited to providing overhead light, its decorative treatment plays a vital role in the aesthetics of the room. Architectural features can establish the dominant mood. Surface treatment can enhance the decorative theme while subtly influencing the mood and even the perception of dimensions.

Wall covering Like paint, a wallpaper treatment on the ceiling can play visual tricks with the dimensions of a room. For added height, look for a small pattern of monochromatic light shades. A linear pattern installed across the width of the room will make it seem wider. For use anywhere in a kitchen, wall covering must be coated and sealed to allow ordinary grease and soil to be scrubbed away without harm to the paper. Such a coating can be applied to the paper of your choice, or you can select a paper that already has a sealer.

Metal A tin ceiling embossed with a decorative pattern and usually painted bestows a genial turn-of-the-century effect. Other metals such as copper or brass also offer stunning, go-for-broke ceiling excitement.

Plaster Plaster, a standard ceiling treatment, offers the options of smooth or textured finish, the former often finished with paint or wallpaper. Plaster also comes mixed with pigment. A heavily textured ceiling mounts some resistance to easy maintenance.

Paint A ceiling's overall effect is often determined by the color value of its paint. Light color values are usually the preferred choice because they are recessive and they reflect light, in effect opening up the room. Dark color values achieve the opposite effect, absorbing light and closing in, for a mood of drama or coziness. Paint gloss adds another variable to the equation. High-gloss paint increases light reflection while also calling attention to blemishes in the plaster. With flat paint, the reverse is true. Semi-gloss paint is a popular middle-ground choice.

Wood The soft texture of a tongue-and-groove wood ceiling lends a friendly element of reassuring intimacy to any kitchen. To the antiseptic functionalism of some ultra-modern kitchens, the warmth of wood overhead may provide a welcome counterbalance. The line of the wood will emphasize the length or width of the room, whichever plane it follows. Painted wood is a lovely ceiling technique, especially where there are rough-sawn beams and tongue-and-groove planks. Paint makes the most of wood's texture without a corresponding heaviness.

Beams Beams almost inevitably lend character to a room, adding interest and vitality by breaking up the overhead plane. Crude, heavy structural beams set parallel or even perpendicular will reinforce a rustic country mood. An open ceiling exposing the entire beamwork and rafters creates a massiveness overhead that demands equivalent treatment on the plane below. Polished, smooth, finely detailed beams contribute the formality of traditional decor. False beams offer clever concealment for ungainly ductwork or even lighting fixtures. Whatever style the beams express, their size must suit the scale of the room.

Windows

Windows channel those vital elements of the outdoors—natural light and fresh air—into the kitchen while framing the garden vistas around your home. The style of the windows should, of course, complement the theme of the kitchen and still be compatible with those elsewhere in the house. Double- or even triple-glazing is crucial on all styles, especially in cold climates, to cut heat loss up to 50 percent. The material of the window sash is more of an architectural than an energy concern. More heat is lost with a metal sash than with wood, but it is minimal when compared to heat lost through the glass.

The following discussion explores the features of movable windows available today. This does not include leaded glass, a popular decorative measure, especially when the view is unsightly. Because of its weight, leaded glass is preferred for stationary installation.

Louvers These horizontal glass panes set into metal frames crank open to provide thoroughgoing ventilation. They offer poor insulation against the cold, however, and cannot be secured against intruders—factors that limit the appeal of these windows.

Bay A bay window forms a glass-enclosed niche extending a room, often into the garden. Always an appealing architectural feature, a bay window can be built to specification or purchased ready-made in units designed to fit standard window openings.

Casement Usually operated by a hand crank, casement windows swing out or inward on vertical hinges. Casement windows are commonly found in bay windows.

Double Hung Double hung windows consist of panes framed in wood or metal that slide up and down in their sashes. Wood frames prevail in older homes; metal frames are more common in new construction.

Sliding Framed in wood or metal, these windows slide open to the side, making them an agreeable choice for a pass-through serving counter between the kitchen and the patio.

French Generally found in casement, bay, and double hung windows, French windows are comprised of panes of glass outlined by wood mullions, creating a geometric patterning pleasing to the eye.

Greenhouse Windows

An all-glass greenhouse window lined with shelves of plants and herbs makes an attractive addition to any kitchen, increasing natural light while expanding the feeling of space. Greenhouse windows come ready-made for easy installation in standard window openings or custom-built to specification. A solarium—or sun room—is merely a greenhouse window turned into a whole room. A solarium extending from the kitchen is a favored choice for the eating nook or indoor garden.

If the solarium will add square footage, the existing structure will have to be modified, and a foundation will have to be laid. The glass should be thermally treated—usually double-glazed—to minimize heat loss; vents are available for the roof of the solarium that will open automatically in warm weather. A solarium can be an excellent component in a passive solar energy system. If it faces south or west, it will gather heat in the cold months; with proper shade landscaping, it can keep heat down during the hot months.

Custom greenhouse window with wood frame

Prefabricated greenhouse window

Solarium or sun room

Skylights

The popular solution to a dark or gloomy interior, a well-positioned skylight enriches a room with abundant natural light while seeming to lift the ceiling. Skylights are available in a wide variety of prefabricated shapes and sizes, or they can be custom tailored to specific needs.

Doors

The position of doors in a kitchen is fundamental to the flow of traffic through the room and the layout of cabinets and appliances. Well-placed doors route pedestrians away from work areas and open freely without bumping cabinet or appliance doors. Entry doors from the outside are made of solid wood or glass and come in a standard width of 36 inches. Interior doors ordinarily consist of wood veneer over a honeycomb or hollow core. They measure 30 to 36 inches wide. In addition to the standard hinged and sliding glass doors, these specialty types offer practical options for kitchen convenience.

Dutch In recent years Dutch doors to the outside have made a return to popular favor. The top and bottom halves of the door function separately—the top can be opened to sunlight and fresh air while the bottom stays shut, confining small children or pets.

Pocket A pocket door of wood or decorative screens separates interior spaces by deftly sliding out on a track from its pocket recess between the studs in the wall. Pocket doors offer the convenience of a nonswinging portal, so crucial in a kitchen, because they don't interfere with traffic patterns or the layout. The wall cavity must clear all wiring and pipes, however. Pocket doors that meet in the middle require less clearance than standard pocket doors.

French The mullioned counterpart of French windows, these doors are usually framed in wood. They are available in sliding units or, more commonly, hinged to swing inward.

Moldings

Moldings provide decorative concealment for graceless joints and crooked edges. Molding style can be simple or extravagant, depending on the decor. Molding materials include wood; Corian; laminated plastic or metal, which can be shaped to conform to the edge; and tile, which can be cut to finish off a curved edge or surface. Counters, backsplashes, cabinet tops, door frames, floors, windows, and so on must often be finished off with some sort of edging to conceal rough edges and irregularities, and a variety of moldings serve that purpose. Choosing moldings is usually an aesthetic consideration—imported tiles, for example, often have no trim, so another material must be used for molding.

Wood molding

Painted wood molding around windows and door

Rounded wood molding

Wood

Tile

Corian

Hardware

Pulls, knobs, and hinges come in an impressive array of materials, including brass, pewter, wood, steel, copper, wrought iron, plastic, and ceramic. Appropriate cabinet hardware is central to a kitchen's overall effect. Those little knobs and pulls may seem inconspicuous, but they are the cabinets' jewelry, enhancing the decorative theme.

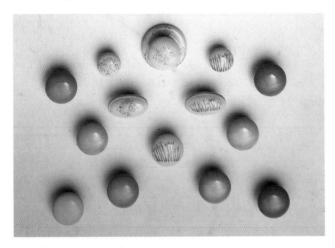

Porcelain cabinet pulls

Traditional metal and porcelain cabinet pulls

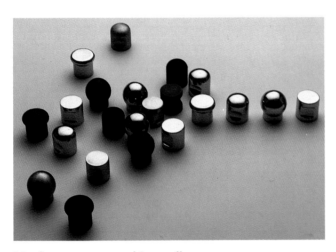

Metal contemporary cabinet pulls

Nylon contemporary cabinet pulls

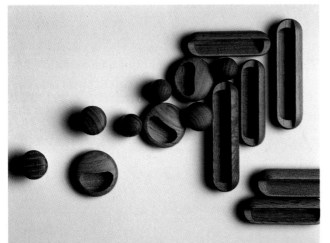

Wood contemporary cabinet pulls

Lighting

Artificial lighting is an essential element of any kitchen, giving vital illumination to work centers and influencing the kitchen's ambience. An electrician can wire lighting fixtures directly into the structure of the kitchen during the framing stage of construction. Alternatively, fixtures can be mounted to finished surfaces and plugged into nearby sockets. If possible, it is helpful to plan for surface-mounted fixtures in advance, so that appropriate outlets and mounting points can be supplied before finish work is completed.

Undercabinet Fixtures These fluorescent fixtures are mounted on the underside of wall cabinets—usually behind a baffle—to illuminate the counter surface below. They can be structurally mounted and wired through the wall with a separate wall switch operating each bank of lights. Or they can be mounted on the surface and operated by individual fixture switches. Some surface-mounted units come equipped with plugs so that fixtures can be connected electrically to one another over a large counter surface without using a wall outlet for each fixture.

Track Lighting Tracks fitted with movable canisters are a flexible lighting method. The canisters themselves come in a selection of colors and styles. Furnished with floodlight bulbs, they provide plentiful overhead illumination; spotlight bulbs serve as accents in the room. On a single track, several canisters can direct light in whatever direction it is needed. The tracks themselves can be recessed into the ceiling or beams, or—less attractive—mounted on the ceiling surface and plugged into a socket.

Box Beams Hollow, surface-mounted beams provide a housing for fluorescent tubes wired into the structure of the ceiling and covered by diffuser panels. Box beams combine the advantages of bright overhead lighting with the decorative appeal of beams.

Ceiling Fixtures The old standard surface-mounted lighting attachments are still available in a generous assortment of styles and sizes.

Indirect Lighting Indirect lighting usually consists of some form of structurally mounted fixture, concealed from view, which casts its light by reflecting off a light-colored surface. Indirect lighting is often installed above wall cabinets. The hidden light shines upward, bouncing off the ceiling to furnish subdued general illumination to the room. Indirect lighting fixtures can also be installed behind crown molding.

Luminous Ceiling This "ceiling of light" consists of fluorescent tubes attached to the ceiling at intervals of about 18 inches. The ceiling is soffited and dropped so that diffuser panels of opaque glass or plastic cover the fixtures and distribute the light evenly. Luminous ceiling fixtures provide exceptionally bright general lighting. Warm white fluorescent tubes are recommended for this application because they are more complementary to the natural colors of food than the cool white type of bulb.

Soffit Lighting Recessed fixtures built into a soffit can supply task lighting over the sink or, extending out beyond the wall cabinets, they cast light down into cabinet interiors and onto counters. Another application is a soffit dropped down over an island and fitted with fluorescent bulbs and diffuser panels to create an overhead radiance illuminating the work area.

Hanging Fixtures These types of lighting devices are suspended from the ceiling, often centered over the dining table. Prudence dictates planning the placement of the table in advance so that the hanging fixture can be mounted in the correct position.

Recessed Fixtures For discreet general overhead lighting, recessed fixtures are a pleasing choice, available in many sizes and shapes. Recessed lights are built right into the ceiling; the housing attaches to the joists either directly or via extension arms.

Appliances

State-of-the-art kitchen appliances are marching to the beat of rapidly advancing technology. Sophisticated electronics and computer wizardry have contributed the most astonishing innovations to formerly humble equipment: touchpad cooktop controls with digital readouts, solid-state sensing devices that register food readiness, lighted refrigerator display panels that visually indicate malfunctions, built-in ice cream makers, appliances with computer voices. . . . The information that follows makes no attempt to keep up with this mad pace of invention, covering only the general features of kitchen appliances. Visit your appliance dealer for an up-to-the-minute briefing on the latest marvels of modern machines.

Surface Cooking Units
Cooktops, set flush with the countertop, offer conventional gas or electric conduction cooking, or induction type. The latter functions via an electromagnetic field created between the electrical source—generally a smooth glass or ceramic surface—and the metal cooking utensil. The electromagnetic field transfers the energy directly to the food. The cooking surface gets warm only from the heat of the food itself, which markedly simplifies cleanup, as spills are not cooked onto the surface.

Induction cooking tiles

Combination gas and electric

Gas

Smooth-top electric

Conventional electric cooktop with grill

Ranges

Each of these cooking units contains a cooktop surface plus one or two ovens. They are available as freestanding or drop-in models and suit wide-ranging needs. They come in widths of 21, 24, 30, 36, and 40 inches. Space-saving units often combine several appliances into one.

Drop-in

Freestanding

Bi-level freestanding

Space-saving range with dishwasher

Ovens

Separate ovens enclosed in coordinated cabinetry satisfy the needs of most kitchen layouts, especially when a separate baking center is part of the overall scheme. Ovens operate on any of the following energy principles. In a gas oven, a burner heats the oven cavity. An electric oven has electrical elements above and below for baking and broiling, respectively. A microwave unit emits radio waves that penetrate the food, causing a molecular reaction that cooks the food. A convection oven utilizes a fan to circulate heated air throughout the oven cavity.

In addition to the conventional oven interior, which requires old-fashioned elbow grease (aided by noxious chemicals) to be kept clean, wondrous new cleaning features are also available. A pyrolytic or self-cleaning oven magically disintegrates food spills at high temperature. In a catalytic or continuous cleaning oven, a catalyst inhabiting the oven walls reacts to and decomposes spills whenever the oven cavity is heated.

Single ovens set into cabinet (convection/microwave above, conventional below)

Microwave oven

European double ovens

Conventional double ovens

Commercial Cooking Appliances

With the increasing sophistication of home cooking has come a trend toward using restaurant ranges, cooktops, and refrigerators in the home. These units provide much more versatility and precise temperature control and facilitate higher-volume use than standard residential models. However, the large size of these units necessitates special layout planning, in addition to heat and noise insulation and specially adapted ventilation.

Ranges offer up to twelve extra-large burners (which accommodate oversized cookware without crowding) and two extra-wide ovens, in addition to grills, griddles, and hot tops (flat metal surfaces for slow cooking). Most commercial ranges operate on gas—though some models are electric—and need heavy-duty up-draft ventilation. Because of the high volume of heat these units put out, they must be surrounded by heat retardant materials such as brick or tile, and no more than six burners are recommended for residential use. Some gas models offer the desirable energy-saving feature of electric ignition.

Cooktops offer similarly versatile surface cooking features. One of these is the hot top, a smooth metal surface for extremely low cooking temperatures that otherwise would not be possible with commercial equipment. All commercial cooktops should be built into insulated, heat-retardant wells.

Range

Cooktop

Hot top

Warming Drawer

A temperature-controlled drawer set for crisp or moist helps to keep food hot and delectable until the moment of serving.

Ventilation

Removing the unpleasant fumes and smoke produced by cooking makes the kitchen more pleasant for its users and helps keep the room clean. All ventilation systems consist of a fan, an exhaust duct, and often a hood to capture fumes and conceal the motor. A system is rated according to the number of cubic feet of air it can exhaust per minute (CFM). A cooktop or range positioned against the wall needs a 400 to 450 CFM vent (the wall aids in guiding the fumes up and away). A peninsula installation requires extra power—900 CFM—and an island needs as much as 1,000 CFM.

Special appliances such as a charcoal grill or a restaurant range add to the burden on the ventilation system, often requiring a custom hood with motor power adapted to the needs of the equipment.

A ventilation system operates most efficiently with a short, straight duct to the outside. Every extra foot of distance and every bend in the route decreases effectiveness and may even necessitate a higher CFM rating.

By far the most common type of system is up-draft ventilation, which captures fumes in a hood and exhausts them up and out through the ceiling. Standard hoods are manufactured ready to install, with fan, motor, and lights that shine down to illuminate the cooktop. For a wall installation, the hood is usually finished only on the one side that is exposed. European designers have devised low-profile wall hoods that blend into the cabinetry; they pull out, slide out, or tilt out for use. A peninsula hood is mounted on the wall or cabinet on one side and is finished on the three exposed sides. An island hood is attached at the ceiling and finished on all four sides. For aesthetic reasons, an island hood may be used over a peninsula. Special decorative effects can be achieved through the design of a custom hood, constructed of almost any material, but often of wood, plaster, brick, metal, tile, or some combination of these materials.

The alternative to up-draft ventilation is a down-draft system, which sucks air and fumes down through the cooking unit and exhausts them through the wall or floor to the outside. Because it does not require an overhead hood, a down-draft system enhances the unobstructed flow of space.

Warming drawer

Conventional wall hood

European pull-out wall hood

Down-draft ventilation

Custom ventilation unit for commercial equipment

Refrigeration

Refrigeration systems include the standard refrigerator—either freestanding or built into a cabinet—and freezer in big stand-alone, little undercounter, or refrigerator-freezer combination models. Refrigerators and freezers today come in frost-free as well as manually defrosting models.

Freestanding side-by-side refrigerator-freezer

Built-in full refrigerator and freezer with trim kit

Side-by-side built-in refrigerator and freezer

Undercounter freezer

Wine cooler

Dishwashers

Dishwashers have advanced from their original, space-consuming built-in model to styles that fit into surprisingly small spaces. The conventional built-in front-loading type continues to be a preferred choice, now available with trim kits to match cabinetry. Its sister model is a top-loading portable that rolls out from its storage place to hook up at the sink. Some portable dishwashers have butcher block tops that permit their use as mobile food preparation islands. The portable model is also produced as a front-loading convertible unit that can be installed in a cabinet as the occasion arises. Space-saving requirements have now inspired a compact model, only 18 inches wide, and combination units offering dual purpose sink-and-dishwasher or cooktop-oven-dishwasher.

Standard-width dishwasher

Compact dishwasher

Built-in Appliances and Accessories

A streamlined solution to the problem of small-appliance clutter consists of little housings in the walls and cabinets surrounding countertop work surfaces.

Paper Storage A paper storage container fitted into the wall between studs provides streamlined housing for foil, plastic wrap, paper towels, etc.

Toaster Wired by an electrician, a toaster can slip neatly into a recess between studs in the wall. It can be positioned at counter height or lower, within easy reach of youngsters.

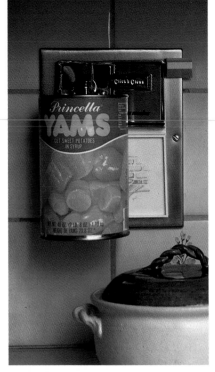

Can Opener A built-in can opener requires professional wiring. It attaches to a stud above the counter at a height designed to allow a tall can to fit easily underneath.

Coffee Maker The coffee maker's housing must be tailored to its height requirements. During the rough construction on the kitchen, a plumber and electrician must stub out a water line and outlet to supply its functioning needs.

Built-In Food-Processing Center For a multipurpose food center, a single-motor unit powers the food processor, mixer, grinder, and blender attachments.

Trash Disposal

Disposition of refuse has not escaped design attention and innovation. Options now include deep, pull-out trash disposal drawers that slide out of base cabinets on glides, a tilt-out style of drawer, a model that hangs on a cabinet door with a cover that pops up when the door is opened and fits hygenically back in place when the door is closed, and a mobile trash disposal unit on wheels that can be rolled to the spot in the kitchen where it is needed. Custom models offer two containers—one for regular trash and a second for recyclable refuse.

Trash container hanging on cabinet door

Pop-up trash compartment

Roll-out trash compartment

Mobile steel trash can on wheels

Pull-out trash compartment

Double built-in compartments for recycling

Compactors

A compactor is an appliance for families that generate a large amount of garbage and/or for those who live in areas not serviced by trash collection agencies. A compactor compresses the trash to a fraction of its uncompressed size. It is available in widths of 12, 15, and 18 inches. Choice is usually influenced by available space, amount of trash generated, and pick-up schedule.

Garbage Disposers

Mainstays of most modern kitchens, garbage disposers are available in two basic types: continuous fed and batch fed. As these terms suggest, continuous-fed disposers can handle food waste fed in continuously, while batch-fed models must be stopped between batches of garbage.

Although garbage disposers have long been common kitchen appliances, they are not suitable for—or even legal in—all areas of the country. They are not recommended, for instance, in communities that rely on septic tanks instead of sewer systems.

Sinks

In recent years sinks have risen from humble utilitarian origins to become decorator items. Stainless steel, copper, brass, porcelain, or space-age plastic in a wondrous range of colors complement or accent almost any decorative palette. Basins now vary in number (single, double, triple), shape (square, oval, or circular), and depth. A common practical choice is a two-compartment sink with one smaller basin for vegetable preparation (housing the garbage disposer) and one larger basin for oversized cookware. Sinks come in both self-rimming and traditional set-in models. Self-rimming sinks have a flange rim that mounts directly on the countertop for easy installation and cleaning. The traditional type is mounted into the countertop, the edge finished with countertop material.

Triple-compartment stainless steel sink

Double-compartment sink for corner installation

Standard porcelain sink with two compartments

Triple sink with molded compartments

Imported stainless steel sink with double oval
compartments

Imported European twin sinks

Single sink with garbage disposer compartment

Single-compartment porcelain sink

Double-compartment porcelain sink with varied bowl size

Round copper sink for vegetable preparation

Stainless steel sink with aprons

Faucets and Sink Accessories

Sink selection does not end with the choice of bowls, finishes, and configurations. Faucets must be chosen from an expanding array of chrome, brass, and metal with porcelain, each of handsome design and efficient function.

In addition to its faucet(s), a sink can also house a spray device, an instant hot water tap, and a water purifier. The sink must be ordered with the exact number of holes required for each accessory. If a dishwasher is part of the kitchen layout, it requires an extra hole in the sink for its air gap.

Brass faucet

European faucet

Reversible single-control faucet with high-arching spout

Single-mix faucet with spray, instant hot water, and water purifier accessories

Flexible single-mix European faucet with instant hot water and water purifier

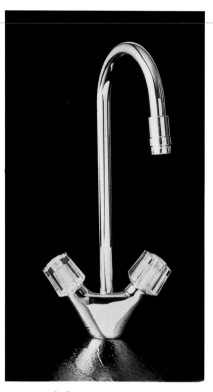

Gooseneck faucet

Adjustable-height faucet

MANUFACTURERS

The following manufacturers can direct you to distributors in your area.

APPLIANCES

Acme National Refrigerator Company
19–26 Hazen Street
Astoria, NY 11105

Admiral Corporation
1701 E. Woodfield Road
Schaumberg, IL 60172

Amana Refrigeration, Inc.
Amana, IA 52204

Caloric Corporation
Topton, PA 19526

Chambers Corporation
Old Taylor Road
Oxford, MS 38655

Everpure, Inc.
660 N. Blackhawk Drive
Westmont, IL 60559

Fasar Systems, Inc.
2801 Burton Avenue
Burbank, CA 91504

Frigidaire Division, G.M.C.
300 Taylor Street
Dayton, OH 45442

Gaffers & Sattler, Inc.
4851 S. Alameda Street
Los Angeles, CA 90058

Gaggenau USA Corporation
150 H New Boston Street
Woburn, MA 01801

General Electric Company
Appliance Division
Appliance Park
Louisville, KY 40225

Hobart Corporation (Kitchenaid)
Troy, OH 45374

In-Sink-Erator
Division of Emerson Electric Company
4700 21st Street
Racine, WI 53406

Jenn-Air Corporation
3035 Shadeland Avenue
Indianapolis, IN 46226

Litton Microwave Cooking Products
1405 Xenium Lane
Minneapolis, MN 55441

Magic Chef, Inc.
740 King Edward Avenue
Cleveland, TN 37311

Modern Maid Division
McGraw-Edison Company
P.O. Box 1111
Chattanooga, TN 37401

Nutone Scoville
Madison and Red Bank Roads
Cincinnati, OH 45227

O'Keefe & Merritt Company and Tappan Company
Tappan Park
P.O. Box 606
Mansfield, OH 44901

Ronson Corporation
1 Ronson Road
Ogletown, DE 19702

Scotsman
505 Front Street
Albert Lea, MN 56007

Sub-Zero Freezer Company, Inc.
P.O. Box 4130
Madison, WI 53711

Thermador
Division of Norris Industries
5119 District Boulevard
Los Angeles, CA 90040

U-Line Corporation
8900 North 55th Street
P.O. Box 23220
Milwaukee, WI 53223

U.S. Range Company
Division of ALCO Foodservice Equipment Company
14501 S. Broadway
Gardena, CA 90248

Vent-A-Hood Company
P.O. Box 426
Richardson, TX 75080

Waste King
Division of Norris Industries
5119 District Boulevard
Los Angeles, CA 90040

Whirlpool Corporation
Administration Center U.S. 33 North
Benton Harbor, MI 49022

White-Westinghouse Corporation
930 Fort Duquesne Boulevard
Pittsburgh, PA 15222

Wolf Range Company
19600 S. Alameda Street
Compton, CA 90224

SINKS

American Standard, Inc.
P.O. Box 2003
New Brunswick, NJ 08903

Delta Faucet Company
P.O. Box 31
Greensburg, IN 47240

Eljer
Division of Wallace-Murray Corporation
3 Gateway Center
Pittsburgh, PA 15222

Elkay Manufacturing Company
2222 Camden Court
Oak Brook, IL 60521

Franke, Inc.
Kitchen Systems Division
212 Church Road
North Wales, PA 19454

Jensen-Thorsen Corporation
301 Interstate Road
Addison, IL 60101

Kohler Company
Kohler, WI 53044

Moen
Division of Stanadyne
377 Woodland Avenue
Elyria, OH 44035

Villeroy & Boch
P.O. Box 103 DW
Pine Brook, NJ 07058

FAUCETS

Chicago Faucet Company
2100 S. Nuclear Drive
Des Plaines, IL 60018

Delta Faucet Company
Division of Masco Corporation of Indiana
P.O. Box 40980
55 E. 111th Street
Indianapolis, IN 46280

Elkay Manufacturing Company
2222 Camden Court
Oak Brook, IL 60521

Grohe
Division of Flygt Corporation
1591 Elmhurst Road
Elk Grove Village, IL 60007

Kohler Company
Kohler, WI 53044

KWC Faucets
Western States Manufacturing Corporation
6900 Eighth Street
Buena Park, CA 90620

Moen
Division of Stanadyne
377 Woodland Avenue
Elyria, OH 44035

Price Pfister
13500 Paxton Street
Pacoima, CA 91331

U.S. Tap
P.O. Box 369
Frankfort, IN 46401

CORIAN

E. I. Dupont & Company
Tatnall Building Products Information Section
Wilmington, DE 19898

LAMINATED PLASTICS

Dura-Beauty
Consoweld Corporation
700 Durabeauty Lane
Wisconsin Rapids, WI 54494

Formica Corporation
120 E. Fourth Street
Cincinnati, OH 45202

Laminart
6430 E. Slauson Avenue
Los Angeles, CA 90040

Nevamar
Division of Exxon Chemical Company
Telegraph Road
Odenton, MD 21113

Wilsonart
600 General Bruce Drive
Temple, TX 76501

TILE

American Olean Tile Company
1000 Cannon Avenue
Lansdale, PA 19446

Country Floors, Inc.
300 E. 61st Street
New York, NY 10021

Designers Tile International
6812 S.W. 81st Street
Miami, FL 33143

Elon, Inc.
964 Third Avenue
New York, NY 10022

Emser International
1660 S. State College Boulevard
Anaheim, CA 92806

International Tile
1288 S. La Brea Avenue
Los Angeles, CA 90019

Latco Products
3371 Glendale Boulevard
Los Angeles, CA 90039

Summitville Tiles, Inc.
Summitville, OH 43962

Walker & Zanger, Inc.
179 Summerfield Street
Scarsdale, NY 10583

FLOORING

Armstrong Company
Liberty and Charlotte Streets
Lancaster, PA 17604

Bruce Hardwood Floors
16803 Dallas Parkway
Dallas, TX 75248

Congoleum Industries, Inc.
195 Belgrove Drive
Kearny, NJ 07032

Connor Forest Industries
P.O. Box 847
Wausau, WI 54401

GAF Corporation
Floor Products Division
1210 Massillon Road
Akron, OH 44305

Kentiles Floors, Inc.
979 Third Avenue
New York, NY 10022

Mannington Mills, Inc.
P.O. Box 30
Salem, NJ 08079
(sheet goods only)

DOORS

Andersen Corporation
P.O. Box 12
Bayport, MN 55003

Customwood
4840 Pan American Freeway N.E.
Albuquerque, NM 87109

Forms & Surfaces, Inc.
P.O. Box 5215
Santa Barbara, CA 93108

Georgia-Pacific Corporation
133 Peachtree Street, N.E.
Atlanta, GA 30303

Louisiana-Pacific
1300 S.W. Fifth Avenue
Portland, OR 97201

Pella Doors
100 Main Street
Pella, IA 50219

WINDOWS

Andersen Corporation
P.O. Box 12
Bayport, MN 55003

Caradco Windows & Doors
Division of Scoville Manufacturing Company
1098 Jackson Street
Dubuque, IA 52001

Lord & Burnham
P.O. Box 225
Irvington, NY 10533

Marvin Windows
Warroad, MN 56763

Pella Windows
100 Main Street
Pella, IA 50219

Southern Cross Lumber & Millwork
143 Brown Road
Hazelwood, MO 63042

LIGHTING

Halo Lighting Division
McGraw-Edison Company
400 Busse Road
Elk Grove Village, IL 60007

Lightolier
346 Claremont Avenue
Jersey City, NJ 07305

Trak Liting, Inc.
14625 E. Clark Avenue
City of Industry, CA 91746

WALL COVERING AND PAINT

The following companies offer customer literature.

Ameritone Paint
P.O. Box 190
Long Beach, CA 90801

Laura Ashley
714 Madison Avenue
New York, NY 10021

Charles Barone, Inc.
9505 W. Jefferson Boulevard
Culver City, CA 90230

Clarence House
111 Eighth Avenue, Room 801
New York, NY 10011

Du Pont De Nemours
1007 Market Street
Wilmington, DE 19898

Fashion Wallcoverings
4005 Carnegie Avenue
Cleveland, OH 44103

General Tire & Rubber Company
979 Third Avenue
New York, NY 10022

S. M. Hexter
2800 E. Superior Avenue
Cleveland, OH 44114

F. Schumacher & Company
939 Third Avenue
New York, NY 10022

Sinclair Paints & Wallcoverings
2500 S. Atlantic Boulevard
Los Angeles, CA 90040

Albert Van Luit & Company
4000 Chevy Chase Drive
Los Angeles, CA 90039

CEILINGS

Armstrong Company
Liberty and Charlotte Streets
Lancaster, PA 17604

Architectural Wood Ceilings
3070 Kerner Boulevard, Suite S
San Rafael, CA 94901

Integrated Ceilings, Inc.
11500 Tennessee Avenue
P.O. Box 64750
Los Angeles, CA 90064

CABINETS

Allmilmo Corporation
P.O. Box 629
Fairfield, NJ 07006

Kemper & Quaker Maid
701 S. N Street
Richmond, IN 47374

Millbrook
Route 20
Nassau, NY 12123

Mutschler
302 S. Madison Street
Nappanee, IN 46550

Riviera Kitchens
Dept. KBB-7, Suite 200
825 Greenbriar Circle
Chesapeake, VA 23320

Poggenpohl USA Corporation
P.O. Box 10 KB2
Teaneck, NJ 07666

H. J. Scheirich Company
P.O. Box 37120
Louisville, KY 40233

SieMatic Corporation
P.O. Box 2536
Santa Barbara, CA 93118

St. Charles Manufacturing
Company
1611 E. Main Street
St. Charles, IL 60117

Wood-Mode Cabinetry
Kreamer, PA 17833

CABINET STORAGE ACCESSORIES

Amerock Corporation
4000 Auburn Street
Rockfield, IL 61101

Feeny Manufacturing Company
P.O. Box 1130
616 Mulberry Street
Muncie, IN 47305

Grant Hardware
High Street
West Nyack, NY 10994

Háfele America Company
P.O. Box 1590
High Point, NC 27261

TAMBOUR PANELS

Forms & Surfaces
P.O. Box 5215
Santa Barbara, CA 93108

Outwater Industries
P.O. Box 1411
Passaic, NJ 07055

Ralph Wilson Plastics Company
600 General Bruce Drive
Temple, TX 75601

HARDWARE

Artistic Brass
4100 Ardmore Avenue
South Gate, CA 90280

Belwith International, Ltd.
7600 Industry Avenue
P.O. Box 1057
Pico Rivera, CA 90660

Forms & Surfaces
P.O. Box 5215
Santa Barbara, CA 93108

Home Hardware
1900 E. Orangethorpe Avenue
Fullerton, CA 92631

The Ironmonger
446 N. Wells
Chicago, IL 60610

Paul Associates
155 E. 55th Street
New York, NY 10022

Valli & Colombo, Inc.
1540 Highland Avenue
Duarte, CA 91010

MOLDINGS

Focal Point, Inc.
2005 Marietta Road
Atlanta, GA 30318

Fypon, Inc.
108 Hill Street
Stewartstown, PA 17363

Maple Brothers, Inc.
1295 W. Lambert Road
Brea, CA 92621

Western Wood Products Association
Yeon Building
Portland, OR 97204

SKYLIGHTS, GREENHOUSES, AND SUN ROOMS

Four Seasons Solar Products Corporation
425 Smith Street
Farmingdale, NY 11735

Lord & Burnham
P.O. Box 255
Irvington, NY 10533

Ventarama Skylight Corporation
140 Cantiague Rock Road
Hicksville, NY 11801

INDEX

The following designers and architects planned the kitchens on the pages indicated:

Carol Belz, ASID 102–3; 141, lower right; 156, lower right

Leonard A. Bergman 8; 17, upper right; 18; 68, lower right; 76, upper middle; 77, upper middle and lower right; 132, upper right; 136, lower left; 137, upper right and lower middle; 140, center of page and lower middle; 168, upper right

Susan Bower 65, upper and lower; 95, upper; 132, lower middle; 138, lower; 156, middle left

Sandra D. Costa 38; 48; 55, lower right; 133, upper middle; 150, upper right

Linda Cracchiolo 41; 49, upper; 167, lower middle

Suzanne Fairly 65, upper and lower; 95, upper; 132, lower middle; 138, lower; 156, middle left

James Geisler 114–5; 132, lower right; 170, middle left

Lily Gelb 3, lower; 20; 31, upper; 55, lower left; 113; 119; 134, upper middle; 135, lower left; 149, upper left; 151, upper right; 167, lower right; 168, lower

Arlene Genis, Designers Circle, Ltd. 14, upper; 21; 120, upper right; 123, lower left; 135, upper middle; 153, upper middle

Orren Harris 14, upper; 21; 120, upper right; 123, lower left; 135, upper middle; 153, upper middle

Steve Hausz 65, upper and lower; 95, upper; 132, lower middle; 138, lower; 156, middle left

Illya Hendrix and Thomas G. Allardyce, Hendrix/Allardyce, A Design Corporation 11, right; 26, left; 37, lower; 39; 52, upper and lower left; 54; 117; 123, lower right; 135, center of page; 141, upper middle; 146, lower right; 155, upper middle and right; 159, lower middle; 166, upper right; 167, lower left

Diane Johnson Design 10, upper right; 31, lower right; 35; 40, upper; 97; 104–5; 110, lower; 120, lower; 133, lower right; 135, lower right; 140, middle right; 149, upper middle; 151, lower right; 152, upper right; 153, lower middle; 155, upper left and lower middle; 171, upper right and lower middle left

Russell K. Johnson ii; iii, left; 10, lower left; 14, lower; 15, upper; 22; 24, right; 68, lower left; 71; 73, lower; 78, upper left; 84, lower right; 90, lower; 91; 96, left; 125; 131, upper left and middle right; 134, lower left and middle; 139, upper middle; 143, upper and lower left; 144, lower right; 145, lower; 146, upper right; 152, lower middle; 154, lower; 158, left; 159, upper middle; 161, upper right; 163, lower left; 164, lower left and right; 170, upper left; 171, lower left

Jeri Katzer 32; 118; 120, upper left; 133, lower middle; 137, middle left and lower right

Lyla Kaufman 67; 152, upper left

Mary Fisher Knott 1; 9; 10, lower right; 11, left; 13; 16; 23, left; 26, right; 29; 40, lower; 43, left and right; 47, upper; 49, lower; 55, upper left and right; 56; 57; 59; 69; 70, lower; 72; 76, upper right, lower left and right; 77, upper and lower left; 78, upper right and lower; 83, upper; 84, lower left; 90, upper; 99; 109; 111, upper left; 121; 123, upper; 131, upper right, lower middle and right, center of page; 132, lower left; 133, lower left; 134, upper and lower right; 135, upper right and lower middle; 136, lower middle; 137, upper and lower left, middle left; 138, middle left; 139, middle left, lower left and middle; 140, upper left; 141, lower middle; 143, lower right; 144, upper and middle right; 145, upper; 146, upper left; 149, upper right; 150, left; 152, upper middle and lower right; 153, middle and lower left, lower right; 158, upper right, upper and lower middle; 159, upper left; 162, lower right; 163, upper and lower right; 164, upper and middle right, lower middle; 167, upper left and middle; 168, upper middle

Ed Kozanlian iii, right; 92–3; 94, left; 106–8; 133, upper left; 142, middle right; 147, lower middle; 162, lower left; 165, lower left; 170, middle right

Judy Lebovich 7, upper; 15, lower; 17, lower right; 27; 83, lower; 94, right; 139, upper right; 146, lower left; 148, upper middle; 151, middle left; 161, lower right; 171, upper middle

H. B. Leydenfrost 9; 16; 121; 144, upper; 162, lower right

Jeffri McAllister, Design Interpretation, Inc. 37, upper; 151, lower left

Bob Miller, Miller-Dupuis Design 109; 111, upper left; 131, upper right; 143, lower right; 145, upper; 150, left; 152 upper middle; 163, upper right; 168, upper middle

Charles Morris Mount 17, upper left; 25; 44–5; 112; 124; 131, lower left; 141, lower left; 147, lower left; 150, lower right; 156, center of page; 158, lower right; 168, upper left

Margy Newman 36; 58; 68, upper; 76, center of page; 85, upper and lower; 136, upper middle and lower right; 137, center of page; 148, lower right; 159, lower left

Luis Ortega ii; 24, right; 91; 131, upper left; 134, lower middle; 143, lower left; 159, upper middle; 164, lower right; 171, lower left

Judith Pacht 70, upper; 89; 137, upper middle

Bruce Colglazier Pappas, PAPPAS 86–8; 114–5; 132, lower right; 142, upper left; 148, lower left; 152, lower left; 170, middle left

Mary Jane Pappas, PAPPAS 86–8; 102–3; 114–5; 132, lower right; 141, lower right; 142, upper left; 148, lower left; 152, lower left; 156, lower right; 170, middle left

Lisa Rose, Aubergine Interiors, Ltd. 19; 74; 76, upper left; 96, right; 131, upper middle; 139, upper left; 144, lower left; 151, center of page; 159, upper right

David Serrurier 12; 47, lower; 52–3; 66; 79; 141, upper left; 149, lower; 154, upper right; 161, upper and lower left; 162, lower middle

Donald E. Silvers, Kitchens by Design 3, upper; 7, lower; 17, lower left; 24, left; 30; 50–1; 63; 73, upper; 76, middle left; 77, upper right; 80–82; 84, upper; 95, lower; 100; 101, upper and lower; 110, upper; 111, middle and lower right; 116; 133, upper right; 134, upper left; 136, center of page and upper right; 138, upper left and right; 140, upper middle and right, lower left; 142, middle left and lower; 144, middle left; 145, middle right; 147, upper left and right, lower right; 148, upper right and lower middle; 153, upper right; 154, upper left; 156, upper right and lower middle; 160, left; 162, upper right; 165, lower middle; 166, lower right; 171, lower right; 172, right

Adele Smolen 31, lower left; 42; 46; 141, upper right; 145, middle left

Irwin N. Stroll, Irwin N. Stroll & Associates 110, upper; 154, upper left

Don Swiers, AIA 60–1; 135, upper left; 142, upper right; 148, upper left; 154, upper middle; 156, middle right

Neil Tidmus 11, left; 26, right; 29; 159, upper left; 163, lower right

Pasquale J. Vazzana 15, upper; 71; 73, lower; 131, middle right; 143, upper; 144, lower right; 154, lower

Claudia Watson, Design Interpretation, Inc. 37, upper; 151, lower left

The following homeowners graciously allowed their kitchens to be photographed for this book:

Teri and Sigmund Abelson
Mr. and Mrs. Merle Amundson
John P. and Linda D. Anderson
Mr. and Mrs. Ralph Bouchey
Susan E. Bower
Dr. and Mrs. Sanford Brotman
Norman Chazin
Jane and Jim Emison
Joshua Freilich
Marjorie and Harold Friedman
Chris Gayner
Lily Gelb
Beth and Merle Gillett
J. Gross
Diane A. and Henry H. Hilton
Dr. and Mrs. Elliott Hinkes
Mary-Jane Iseli
Sam and Sylvia Kaplan
William and Laurie Kasch
Mr. and Mrs. Sheldon Katzer
E. P. Kranitz
Max and Judy Lebovich
George Le Fave
Mr. and Mrs. G. Douglas Lewis
Mr. and Mrs. Ira R. Manson
Harry Marks
Mr. and Mrs. James L. McDonald
Dr. and Mrs. Frank Meronk, Jr.
Lindy Michaels
Accie Mitchell, M.D.
Charles Morris Mount
Dr. and Mrs. Ronald Nelson
Mr. and Mrs. Arnold Newman
Laraine Newman
Judith and Jerry Pacht
John and Rickie Pauldine
Joy and Regis Philbin
Maureen Polich
Bruce Roberts
Judi and Howard Sadowsky
Mr. and Mrs. Richard Schnell
Mr. and Mrs. Bruce Seidel
David Serrurier
Mr. and Mrs. John Stewart
Mr. and Mrs. Larry Stickney
Angel Pierre Unamuño
Claudia Watson
Roberta and Lew Weintraub
Samuel M. Weprin

Photographers: All original photographs by Diane Padys Photography, with assistance by Deborah Jones and prop styling by Robin Murawski and Nan Oshin, except:

Mark Schwartz 61, upper left and lower right; 135, upper left

William P. Steele (prop stylist, Matthias Mattiello) iii, right; 17, upper left; 19; 25; 44–5; 74; 76, upper left; 92–3; 94, left; 96, right; 106–8; 112; 124; 131, upper middle and lower left; 133, upper left; 139, upper left; 141, lower left; 142, middle right; 144, lower left; 147, lower left and middle; 150, lower right; 151, center of page; 156, center of page; 158, lower right; 159, upper right; 162, lower left; 165, lower left; 168, upper left

Jessie Walker (prop stylist, Mary Jane Pappas) 86–8; 102–3; 114–15; 132, lower right; 141, lower right; 142, upper left; 148, lower left; 152, lower left; 156, lower right; 170, middle left

The following manufacturers supplied the photographs on the pages indicated:

Belwith International, Ltd. 157, upper left and right
Elkay Manufacturing Company 169, lower left and right
Forms and Surfaces 157, middle left and right, lower left
Gaggenau USA Corporation 160, upper right
Kohler Company 170, lower left and right; 171, upper right; 172, middle
Magic Chef, Inc. 166, middle
Modern Maid 162, upper middle
Moen 172, right
Nutone Scoville 167, upper right
Sub-Zero Freezer Company, Inc. 165, upper middle and right
Thermador 166, left
U.S. Tap 171, lower middle
Villeroy and Boch 170, upper right
Waste King 169, upper
Whirlpool 162, upper left

For providing accessories, special thanks to Williams-Sonoma, Inc., with stores in Boston; Phoenix; Denver; Dallas; Minneapolis; San Francisco; Los Angeles; San Diego; Beverly Hills, CA; Palo Alto, CA; Costa Mesa, CA; Pasadena, CA; Cupertino, CA; Stamford, CT; Short Hills, NJ; Oakbrook, IL

Additional accessories: 19, Of All Things, New York; 44–5, D. F. Sanders & Company, New York, and Of All Things; 74, Of All Things; 106–8, Phillip Mueller Company, New York, and D. F. Sanders & Company; 112, Of All Things; 124, Of All Things; 141, lower left, Of All Things and D. F. Sanders & Company; 144, lower left, Of All Things; 147, lower left, Of All Things

Special thanks to:
Olivia Buehl, Editor, HOME magazine
Barbara Portsch, Senior Editor, Kitchens/Baths, HOME magazine
Kathy Kowgios, Editorial Assistant, HOME magazine
David M. Smith, Assistant to the Editor, HOME magazine
Anthony P. Iacono, Vice President, Manufacturing, Knapp Communications Corporation
Philip Kaplan, Vice-President, Executive Graphics, Knapp Communications Corporation
Patrick R. Casey, Vice-President, Production, Knapp Communications Corporation
Donna Clipperton, Manager, Rights and Permissions, Knapp Communications Corporation
Faith Haase, Rights and Permissions Coordinator, Knapp Communications Corporation
Sally Kostal
Georgia Griggs
Elaine Linden
Lois Oster
Patrick McHugh

The Knapp Press is a wholly owned subsidiary of **Knapp Communications Corporation.**

Chairman and Chief Executive Officer: Cleon T. Knapp
President: H. Stephen Cranston
Senior Vice-Presidents:
    Rosalie Bruno (New Venture Development)
    Betsy Wood Knapp (MIS Electronic Media)
    Harry Myers (Magazine Group Publisher)
    William J. N. Porter (Corporate Product Sales)
    Paige Rense (Editorial)
    L. James Wade, Jr. (Finance)

The Knapp Press

President: Alice Bandy; *Administrative Assistant:* Beth Bell; *Editor:* Norman Kolpas; *Managing Editor:* Pamela Mosher; *Associate Editors:* Jan Koot, Sarah Lifton, Diane Rossen Worthington; *Assistant Editors:* Colleen Dunn Bates, Nancy D. Roberts; *Art Director:* Paula Schlosser; *Designer:* Robin Murawski; *Book Production Manager:* Larry Cooke; *Book Production Coordinators:* Veronica Losorelli, Joan Valentine; *Director, Rosebud Books:* Robert Groag; *Creative Director, Rosebud Books:* Jeff Book; *Financial Manager:* Joseph Goodman; *Assistant Finance Manager:* Kerri Culbertson; *Financial Assistant:* Julie Mason; *Fulfillment Services Manager:* Virginia Parry; *Director of Public Relations:* Jan B. Fox; *Marketing Assistants:* Dolores Briqueleur, Randy Levin; *Promotions Managers:* Joanne Denison, Nina Gerwin; *Special Sales Manager:* Lynn Blocker; *Special Sales Coordinator:* Amy Hershman